"When we Learn from
Someone Ahead of Us,
&
Teach someone behind Us
The road we are on Now
is so much
Better!"
~GB~

Aerial Approach

(Modern Pioneers)

Inspiring & CONDENSED

MINI LIFE LEGACY STORIES

LOOK UP!

Observing life from an aerial perspective can help the heart to change, and who knows... there may be someone above or ahead of you on the journey. One you hadn't noticed before... just waiting to lend you a helping hand. A pioneer just like you that has the answers to blaze a trail for you and your family. Having a hard time? Use the aerial approach and LOOK UP!

Rich little Stories and lessons from others that help to negotiate or avoid mine fields of life. Some stories are embarrassing, sad, scary, and more. OUR MESS is
OUR MESSAGE.

Aerial Approach

(Modern Pioneers)
Inspiring & CONDENSED
MINI LIFE LEGACY STORIES

Copyright © 2018 G Roai Burnett

All rights reserved
No part of this book may be reproduced, retrieved in a retrieval system, or transmitted by any means, electronic, mechanical, photocopying, recording, or otherwise, without written permission by the copyright holder.

Book Design & Technical layout
G Roai Burnett

**ISBN-13:
ISBN: 978-1726708302
(GRB GLOBAL CREATIONS)**

DEDICATION

As I read the short mini stories I marvel at the powerful and simply illustrated little snippets that draw me closer to my great ancestors, pioneer family, and friends. Insights and perspectives that would not have been discovered had I not pursued this project. It is said that:

"A STORY NOT WRITTEN IS SOON FORGOTTEN."

I reflect back on a presentation given at a large world family history conference in which the presenter invited his family go back and find a relative that they could relate with and that would have an answer to some of the trials or hurdles they might correlate with our modern day lives.

My heart turns to those pioneers, both modern and ancient, who have blazed the trail before us and paved the way today. Many were found by clicking on their names on the family tree.

It was so nice to see that their lives were of great value, even though they might of thought that daily life was very simple, sometimes very difficult, and often times mundane and monotonous. I realized we can learn a lot from each other..

It was fun to share with my family as they were thinking their lives were not all that exciting, but as we hear about it with a little bit of time behind it, we found interesting and fun memories to share with each other.

Thank you to all that participated and contributed to this project.

Please forgive me as the book may contain errors hear and their. Hopefully you'll be able to find many hidden treasures a long the way.

It's about the stories, so thank you in advance for your patients and forgiveness.
A friend use to say to me:

"If at first you don't suck seed,
"keep on sucking until you do suck seed"

(by changing something you can succeed)

...Change is Key
~GB~

FUN LITTLE STORIES
OF
(Modern Pioneers)
Full of
LOVE AND HOPE

Chapter 1

CPR FOR THE SOUL
Nate Hales
pg 15

Chapter 2
I
IT WAS JUST A DRINK

Shock Waves to Others
Aaron Allen
pg 27

Chapter 3

WASTE BASKET ARTIST
Margie Boyle
One Person's Garbage
is Another Person's Treasure
pg 33

Chapter 4

THE PRIZE IN SIR PRIZE
Karissa Burnett
pg 39

Chapter 5

A NEW WAY TO HAVE KIDS
Gary R Burnett
pg 57

Chapter 6

HEALING:
The other side of the veil -
Nora Burnett
pg 71

Chapter 7

DIRT
All families have it!
Michael Burnett
pg 75

Chapter 8

MANY HANDS
Make light work
Bonnie Chadburn
pg 83

Chapter 9

A FEW THINGS TO SAY
About **MOTHERS** and More
Vaneta (Neta) Burnett
pg 89

Chapter 10

FLIPPED A CASKET
Mary Roseltha Fuller Burnett
Rubber necking-
pg 93

Chapter 11

THE ROCKET ROOST
D. Burnett   About Aunt Pauline
pg 103

Chapter 12

LOVE AT HOME
G Roai Burnett
pg 105

Chapter 13

SAVING THE PROPHET'S FATHER
Matthew Burnett
pg 115

Chapter 14

COMING TO A BOOK NEAR YOU
pg 119

(Your name goes here -3 to 5 pages-tell your story)

LIFE LEGACY GAME

[ ] Very limited Editing to preserve original contribution

ACKNOWLEDGMENT &
CONTRIBUTIONS
(Short stories interspersed throughout the book

After compiling the contributions laughter ensued, then tears came to my eyes as I realized how wonderful and insightful these stories are. I had no idea from the many stories shared, especially some from ancestors that have already passed on that left these little snippets about their lives. This was eye opening. Love was increased for each person as conversations about ancestors, people, places and things that made indelible impressions upon our lives. were shared with love and hope.

I appreciate the support and the spirit by those who have written these contributions. Great thanks go to my dear family for the hours and hours of assistance, even from the badgering, or coaxing, telling me "GOOD LUCK WITH THAT" or. the wonderful strong encouragement too because it was all necessary to keep me moving forward and especially sharing the life lessons along with the fond memories. Thank you all!

 It was an honor and a privilege to assemble the contributions into this book and to get it into (digital) print, and especially my older sister for blazing the trail and getting her book completed and allowing me to learn and grow along with her.

~MP~
CHAPTER 1

CPR FOR THE SOUL

Contribution~

*Nate Hales Story
(excerpts from his
CPR for the Soul)*

I am a 43-year-old agent for an insurance company in Utah. I became addicted to heroin and other drugs and began stealing from my father to support this habit. I grew up in a respected Mormon family, in The Church of Jesus Christ of Latter-day Saints (LDS), and desperately wanted to live a cleaner life, but felt powerless over the drugs. Then one day, I walked up a mountain behind my father's house and experienced a transcendent, transforming, life-changing encounter with God that healed my addiction and helped me gain clarity for the first time in my life.

By the age of 23, I was an addict, such a mess. I was taking so many pills — "cousins" to heroin…whatever I could get my hands on. My father is a successful dentist, and I put myself on his payroll, although he didn't notice. I was taking checks out of his mail and cashing them. I stole tens of thousands of dollars from him. His CPA is the one who realized the money was missing.

There is a beautiful movie called Pleasure Unwoven: An Explanation of the Brain Disease of Addiction. It's a documentary DVD produced in 2010 that explains that addicts just can't stop using, stealing and destroying themselves. I highly recommend it to anyone who has an addiction and anyone who is trying to help an addict. I used to walk to the store and steal things, crying because I couldn't stop myself. That's how bad it was. I lost my car, my job and everything else. I just wanted to die because I couldn't stop this body from walking around to commit crimes just to get high again.

I have an identical twin brother, and we have a younger brother. One day, my younger brother called me on the phone and said, "Dad found out you've been stealing money from him. He's on his way over to your house right now."

I had been in jail a few times, and I said, "I am not going to prison. I'm going to Mexico." So I packed a bag and was getting ready to leave. My dad pulled in the driveway and got out of the car. I began to cry, and I looked at him with dark, sorrowful pity. A horrid emptiness engulfed me. I felt like a damned soul. I didn't even believe in God at that time. My dad was the only latch I had to my old life because my twin brother was using drugs, too. And there he was. I didn't want to get close to him because I didn't know if he was going to try to tackle me or keep me from leaving. I just didn't want to go to prison.

I told my dad, "I cannot tell you how sorry I am. You're looking at somebody who's out of control. I am going to go to Mexico, and I will probably die." In my mind, the only way out was to kill myself. In fact, I had already attempted suicide, but my brother stopped me.

Dad's eyes started to fill with tears, and he told me, "No, no! Just calm down. We'll take care of this. We'll work it out. Don't go anywhere; don't do anything. Just come home. You're going to come home. I'm going to get you out of this deep hell you're in, but you're going to live by my rules. And you're going to go to church with me."

What an amazing human he is. I had already failed at rehab several times and stolen maybe $35,000 from him, yet he took me back in, like the Prodigal Son.

I moved back home, and he wanted me to wake up each morning and read Scriptures with him, go to church with him on Sunday and sit in on the family prayers. I wanted to turn my life around, but I just couldn't stop popping the pills. I started lying to my dad again.

One Tuesday evening, I got back to my dad's house after work, and I wanted to go to a bar or a club. I borrowed his truck and drove to a nearby city to pick up a friend of mine, J.P.. He was a pothead. He loved smoking pot and studying Buddhism. He was into different things every week. J.P. loved going against society and the grain. He told me two missionaries were going to be at his house in a little while to talk to him.

I said, "Let's just go!"

He said, "No, if you want me to go to the club with you, you're going to sit here and wait until these guys are done. I've got an appointment with them."

I protested. "Just leave them. These kids are twenty years old. Why are you going to meet with them? Do you just want to mess with them and tell them Santa Claus isn't real? They're not hurting anybody, and they're not addicted to stuff, so leave them alone. You just want to smoke your pot, trip out on them, Bible-bash them and try to take away their faith."

J.P. said, "No, I don't. Just shut up. Get out of here if you don't want to wait for me."

He was the only person who would hang out with me, so I waited. The two missionaries showed up. This kid from Delaware sat down and started talking to J.P.. Then he turned to me and started lighting up — I can't even explain it. He started telling me about Jesus Christ. I had heard it all before because my dad was religious.

"What Kind of Drug Is This?"
But this was incredible. It was powerful. The Spirit was speaking to me. The young missionary told me, "You are going to change. You're going to influence thousands of people. You're going to do great things — I can see it."

He prophesied my life. The room seemed to glow. I wondered if I was tripping on LSD or something because it was so potent. I wondered, "What kind of drug is this? This light and this hope…" It's like I had been in a dark cave, and somebody ripped the top off the cave, and all this light came pouring down on me. It was a beautiful feeling that went clear through me. I knew what he was saying was true.

The Spirit was burning through the room so strongly. The missionary said, "Can you feel that? That's the Spirit!" Caught up in the overwhelming transformation taking place, he stood up and shouted, "I have never felt it this strong! Wahooooo!"

Something in me changed at that moment. I was still addicted to drugs, but my heart started beating again. The missionary told me, "I want you to go to church, even if you're sedated."

I told him, "I can't do that. It's rude to go to church while I'm high."

He disagreed strongly. So I made a commitment that I would keep going to church with my dad on Sundays. There were times when I'd walk into church, even though I had just popped a bunch of pills. I was like, "I'm here. I'm barely here, but I'm here. I'm sorry I'm wasted. I'm sorry I'm high, but I'm here, and I'm going to continue on this pattern. I am going to turn my life around."

My Mountaintop Salvation Experience:

For the next six months, I tried to quit my addiction and be the man I knew I should be. One day, I got off the bus from work and saw an unfamiliar car in front of my dad's house. I thought it was a parole officer. I wondered if maybe I had forgotten to pay a ticket.

I didn't want to find out. It was 5 o'clock in the afternoon, and I decided to go for a walk, up the mountain behind my dad's house. I saw one of our neighbors, and he asked how I was doing. He said, "I see you at church. Listen, I don't know exactly what you're going through, but all I know is that you've got to give it to the Savior."

I asked, "What do you mean?"

He said, "You've just got to ask Him to take it from you."

We talked for about 15 minutes. Then I walked down the road about a mile. There were no houses out there. My dog, Scruffy, was with me. She saw the whole thing. I looked out across the valley. It was pure daylight, and I got on my knees. I had a conversation with God. I said, "I feel like there's something on the other side. I feel these little pieces of gold that have come into my life over the past six months, like what the missionary said to me. But I can't shake this addiction. I know I'm going to go use pills tonight. I know I'm going to go do whatever I can to just get loaded again. I know You can hear me. I can't do it. You've got to take it from me because I can't do it on my own."

I really didn't want to live anymore. I didn't want to disappoint my dad, who was trying to save my life. I figured I was hooked for life and would die an addict.

At that moment, I felt like someone placed hands on my head. I felt the presence of two people, whom I knew. It felt so familiar. As soon as they touched my head, I knew everything was going to be OK. They felt like brothers. I sensed that they had always been there, had always been in charge and were doing the work of God. Everything was clear. I knew Jesus Christ was the Savior. But the sensation I had wasn't of realizing something; it was a sensation of remembering something, and how could I have forgotten that?

I didn't actually see people standing there with me, but I sensed their overwhelming presence. It was the Spirit testifying. You can't testify about truth and not feel its power. I realized a lot of things that day. When it all peeled back, I remembered that God is so involved in our lives as we're doing our everyday things, and we can't see it. But for a moment, I saw it.

For some reason, I had a pen and paper with me, and I wrote down 20 truths, or lessons, God gave me to strengthen me and overcome my addiction. They were things like, "Don't dwell on anything but the truth of God." The truth of God means that you should work hard to support your family. Another truth is that we should talk good about our neighbors instead of talking bad about them. Just doing good unto others. Everything that's worthwhile, that's where you dwell. That's what you put your mind on.

During this mountaintop experience, I saw my addiction clearly — and it cured me. Addicts know what's going on, but they're so scatterbrained. This experience rebuilt my mind. I stopped taking drugs at that moment, and I never even had withdrawals — no shaking, no nothing. I looked out across the valley, and I saw the intricate involvement of heaven pouring through everything. I felt an inextinguishable love and felt how deeply we are all connected. We are certainly never alone.

A New Beginning
After this phenomenal experience, I walked down the mountain, back into my dad's house. He was there, and I asked him who had visited. He said it was a friend of his. It wasn't a cop, like I had feared. He looked at me. He could tell there was something different about me.

I said, "Dad, I'm going to be honest with you. I have continued to do drugs while I've lived here, but it's gone now. I'm telling you, it's all gone!"

I walked toward him and hugged him. I felt so carefree and happy again, like I did when I was 12 years old. Finally, my brain was in the right place. Everything had hope in it again. Life was beautiful. I went to my room and typed out the 20 truths that God had shared with me on the mountaintop — truths that He had custom-tailored just for me. Twenty years later, I still have that list of the 20 keys to my sobriety.

But even though my brain was fixed, I knew I needed to repay the money I owed my dad and begin serving myself and others as I would serve God Himself. I knew I had to take control of my life, or the devil would do so again.

I decided to go on a two-year mission trip to Atlanta for the Mormon church, the LDS church. I wanted to give back. I wasn't married yet, and I didn't have kids yet. The leaders in the church weren't sure they wanted me to be a missionary. They didn't want me relapsing out there, away from home, and setting a bad example for others.

But then one of the top leaders read my file and told me he wanted me to go. He said, "You've been through a lot."

I said, "Yeah."

And he said, "No, you've really been through a lot!" His eyes seemed to look right to the core of my soul. After only a moment, he proclaimed, "You are going to make a great missionary!" The Lord helped him see, without words, the purification of Christ's atonement.

CPR for the Soul

One day, I was talking to my friend, Greg, a phenomenal guy. I stopped him and said, "Hey, Greg. You have some friends who have gone back to using, but you've always stayed good. Your friends kind of fell back into the pit. They're like the pig that eats its own vomit. How can I avoid doing that?"

Greg told me, "You've got to do three things: you've got to show up once a week and meet with other people, talk about God — you've got to go to church. Second, you've got to pray every day. Show some respect — get down on your knees. You can't be lying in bed. It takes maybe ten seconds or thirty seconds. And third, you've got to read just one verse of Scripture every day. It has to be a meaningful one, and a different one every day. You'll never fall too far if you just do those three things and never miss. The Lord loves consistency!"

Then I realized that those three important activities form the acronym CPR: church (every Sunday), prayer (every day, on your knees) and reading Scriptures (at least one per day). I worked three jobs to go on the mission trip in Atlanta. I went out there and shared with people what I know: CPR for the soul — it's the consistency that counts!
Life Is Grace, and Pain Is a Gift
Life is grace. God has put us on this Earth so we can learn. Every bit of pain we go through helps us understand the object and design of our existence, which is happiness. It is only by His grace that we get to be here.

The pain we feel in our lives is a gift. You cannot comprehend the beauty of daylight and sunshine until you've been in Alaska in the wintertime for three months straight, and you come back down to California and see the green grass and feel the warm sunshine.

To anybody in pain, I want to tell you that we are all in the middle of a process. How do we find truth? It's not that hard, but it is a process. We have to build our spiritual "muscle." If you want to do some pull-ups, you don't just start doing a bunch of them right away if you've never done them before. If you try to skip that growth process and ask God to give you strength without going through the pain, then you have missed the whole point of life. Why would the Lord rob us of the process?
Here are just two of many Bible verses that I turn to when I need to feel God's strength:

"But seek ye first the kingdom of God, and his righteousness; and all these things shall be added unto you."

— MATTHEW 6:33

"For every one that asketh receiveth; and he that seeketh findeth; and to him that knocketh it shall be opened."—

MATTHEW 7:8

~MP~
CHAPTER 2

IT WAS JUST A DRINK
-Shock Waves to Others

~*Contribution*~

Aaron Allen

As I drive this road each morning I contemplate on the marks in the ground which almost became the resting spot of a sidewalk wreath. This morning I had a very poignant thought that became the inspiration for the following message. I wish I could express it as I talked, but my tears would stop me from finishing. Please take a few minutes to read and ponder.

A year ago, I had the privilege of celebrating Easter focused on the spiritual message of Christ and his love for his brothers and sisters as I recovered in a hospital bed. I have learned so many lessons as I have suffered through physical pain and spiritual anguish. I have come to know and believe in Christ at a level that has changed my life and forever shapes me as a man, father, spouse, brother, friend, and example.

"I stand all amazed at the love Jesus offers me. Confused at the grace that so fully he proffers me. I tremble to know that for me he was crucified. That for me, a sinner, he suffered, he bled and died. Oh, it is wonderful that he should care for me
Enough to die for me! Oh, it is wonderful, wonderful to me!" (Lds hymn 193)

The night of my accident exactly a year ago is still a blur; however, I vividly still remember the peace and love of Christ and God that I felt as I awoke and regained consciousness. This feeling was so strong and powerful and encompassed my heart. Oh I wish I could describe how deep, soul freeing, and powerful Gods love for you feels as death door knocks.

I strive each day to stay close to this feeling. It changed me. I plead for all who have witnessed the miracle [of] my life to stay close to God. Believe in him. Believe and live your lives loving and forgiving others. The memories and love you shared with others during this life will fast forward in the present as you stand at the door of death. I am privileged to continue to make memories and be there as a friend for countless others while I fulfill the new mission God has for me.

I am doing very well. My physical infirmities are healing, but more importantly my soul is becoming more Christlike. I have shed tears over the year hoping I can be an example of his love and help you to feel his love. I commit to do my part.

God lives. God loves. Jesus is the Christ and will come again. I can't wait to cry at his feet and say Thank you, Thank you, Thank you!!! I LOVE YOU! I LOVE YOU! I LOVE YOU!

Easter has forever been changed for me. We will all rise again with our Lord, Master, Friend, Redeemer, and Savior. He suffered, died, and was resurrected for YOU!

(The Story Continues)

Sentencing is over and am able to move on to next chapter in life. Here are the remarks I felt Impressed to share at [the court] sentencing.

Six months ago the car wreck I was involved in changed my life dramatically.

The worries and pain of my physical infirmities will be with me and my family for the rest of my mortal life. The financial burden that my family may face due to my early potential death may become a challenge. The stress and impact on my wife, children, and family the past few months are hard to quantify let alone put into words.

With these challenges it would be very easy to be bitter and vindictive against [this impaired man]. However, from the moment I came to full consciousness a few days after the accident I have felt a different spirit. I found a spirit of gratitude to be alive. I found Jesus Christ's spirit of love and look forward to being with family, friends, and a community that loved me for a few more years. But, Most importantly I found the spirit of Christ's atonement and mercy in forgiving me of my sins and my ability to forgive [this man] for causing some setbacks.

I was humbled by the many prayers offered in my and [the impaired driver's] behalf. My children's and wife's prayers for his recovery touched my heart. We continue to pray for his ability to recovery from alcoholism and pray that he will find peace in following the Lord.

My recovery has been a miracle. The events of that night and the participants placed in the experience were not there by coincidence . I stand before the court this day to boldly exclaim that Heavenly Father, Jesus Christ, and the Holy Spirit are real. There is life after death. The peace and love in that location are worth living a good life on the earth. My life's mission is to be an example of Christs love for all others to feel. I will go to my grave helping others know that they are unconditionally loved by the Lord.

 [Looking to the drunk driver:] Please take this time of temporary setback and put your life in the ultimate direction you want it to go. Honor the men and women in your life that love you and prove to them that you can live a life full of love and compassion.

Thanks to my family members, doctors, and nurses who spent many nights tending to me and helping me recover from the many injuries. Finally thanks to my dear wife who has been by my side through this entire experience. I will be forever indebted to her and the example she set for our beautiful three children. Her name will be honored and revered for eternity.

~MP~
CHAPTER 3

WASTE BASKET ARTIST
One person's garbage is another person's treasure.
Grandma Margie Boyle

Life history of Margaret May Warner Boyle

Was born on March 16, 1917, in a small single house on 20th St, a block from Washington Boulevard. We lived about a block from town, a short walk to the center of town. The little house is still there, but I was born in. When I was born. The doctor failed to register my birth with the state and legally I was nobody until I had to obtain a passport for travel later on. Then I had to do considerable research in order to obtain a birth certificate.

My dad, James Livet Warner was a dedicated railroad man. He carried a little grip-like suitcase, and we would always run to see what he brought home for a treat. It was usually pack [of gum]. The neighborhood kids always liked him real well because he was generous with his gum.

Dad spent four days on the railroad and two days at home continuously until his retirement, after 51 years of service. He was extremely loyal and faithful employee and would not allow us children to say anything negative about the railroad claiming. "We should not bite the hand that fed us." They gave him a nice TV when he retired. They had his picture in the railroad magazine with a nice write up.

Dad collected , diamonds, but it didn't do him much good because they were all stolen. When they came home in 1939. Someone had ransacked their home and taken all their valuables.

My dad was 30 years old when he married mother, who was 20. My mother, Margaret Elizabeth Harbertson Warner, was a tremendous homemaker. She had a strong testimony of the truthfulness of the gospel. She had a little library church books. She would bring some of them out to renew her memory of the Scriptures.

My mother was an excellent cook and so was my dad. I remember their homemade stew and soup and Chile, and mothers pies and cakes. Mother could make the best layer cakes I ever tasted. It was like velvet. Dad was an expert on stews and soup.

My parents would take me, when I was in the only child, to the vaudeville and show at the old Orpheum theater, and to dinner afterwards.

I had two boy brothers die in infancy. One in 1918, Lester Lamar Warner of the flu, which was a terrible epidemic in the city at that time, and children were dying like flies. My parents, myself and the baby all had this flu, and they said it was a blessing that I ever survived. Two years later, Ray Harbertson Warner arrived. He was a healthy, beautiful baby. At 4 1/2 months. He died after the doctor lanced his ear after he had a sudden earache.

Mother was terribly upset at this, and was too nervous to stay alone, so we moved to grandma Harbertson's home. We stayed a year until she was able to face life again. That year, remains in my memory as a very choice experience, including sleeping on a feather bed and also having my Christmas sock hop on their old-fashioned wall telephone by their big heatrola in their dining room. On the side of the dining room was couch fitted with a feather bed mattress with which I sunk into literally, and greatly enjoyed on the cold winter nights. I had the privilege of becoming very close to my grandparents, whom I consider [to be] the salt of the earth.

My Grandmother, Mary Elizabeth Moffat Harbertson was married to John William Harbertson. Grandma was a [avid] reader, she read all she could get a hold of, and was a refined, sensitive little lady, who was a super cook. She had her own flower garden and presented all of her visitors with a bouquet of her beautiful flowers and [a bowl] of her homemade chili.

Grandpa was a farmer at heart, who [had] choice, vegetables, and [shared this passion] with each of his sons, who built the Harbertson Ford Motor company, located in the northeast corner of Washington Boulevard. On the second floor of that building was a sports arena and a wrestling school. The children included John, James, Brigham, Perl, Mary, Margaret, Edna, and one child that died in birth. Grandpa liked to read and he carried a doctrine and covenants around with him, and he had memorized most of it. He would say, "Margie what chapter would you like me to read." And he would recite it. Uncle Jim invested his money in farmland and he had grandpa Harbertson farm it. He had a farm with cows, horses, and a chicken coop and chickens.

When I was six years old, my sister Lois arrived. She was born in our home at 865 27th St. She was a beautiful, fragile baby who had lots of ear infections. Consequently was a bit spoiled, because mom was a bit cautious because of her previous experience with the baby boys.

At this time in my life. There was a family who moved two doors from us to have three little girls close to my age. Their names, Rosemary, Glenna, and Doris Dee. I was extremely happy with the companionship of these three girls, and brokenhearted when they moved three years later.

I entered the first grade and had a teacher that scared the life out of me the first year. The second year, I had a lot of sickness and was absent from school. The teacher wanted me to repeat the second grade. Mother put her foot down and insisted I would hold my own in the third grade. Evidently I did, as the teacher in the third grade suggested that I skipped the fourth grade, Mother refused. The sixth grade teacher wanted me to skip the seventh grade. She came over to our home and I listened through the crack through the kitchen door. I was very disappointed in this, as I wanted to to be a classmate of my cousin, Jim Lazenby.

Many of my fun experiences as a child, were the picnics that were planned with Aunt Blanche, Aunt Date, and Jim (Aunt Blanches Son). Many enjoyable afternoons were spent at the railroad men's boardinghouse ran by my Aunt Date (my dad's sister, Caroline Warner Lincoln). She was widowed after eight years in Randy's boarding houses for survival. I remember her white linen tablecloths, and her tempting meals served thereon. She was very nice to us when we visited, and always would have us have dinner and send up to the drive-in for a picture of cold root beer to have on her front porch. Once in a while, when I left, she would put a silver dollar in my hand.

When mother had the twins. She was swollen up. After my mother had the babies, that was really shocked when we met him at the door and told him he had twins. He was so thrilled! We had waited until two o'clock in the morning to tell dad when he came home from the railroad.

When I was 12 1/2 years old, we moved to the brand-new home at 2030 Fowler. The homes and in that area. had been purchased by families. One time I counted 90 children on our block, so my life was fun, fun, fun with all the kids, but I don't know about mom and dad's. At this time I made one of my choicest friends, Dorothy Russell. After high school, Dorothy's life was not too happy, and I have completely lost track of her.

In high school art was interesting to me, and I got excellent grades in this subject. [There] was a Christmas lighting contest, and it was [to draw] a large sketch of the first security Bank building, including a Christmas lighting design that I had planned. It really irritated me to draw the sketch. Finally, I just crumpled it up and threw it in the wastebasket. Two weeks later, in the Sunday paper, my dad came into the bedroom and said,
"Look at this!"

I had won first place and a check for $10, included in the letter from the bank. My teacher had retrieved it from the garbage, smoothed it out, and entered it in the contest for me. Boy was I thrilled! I was jumping up and down on the bed!

~MP~
CHAPTER 4

SURPRISE: THE PRIZE IN THE SIR PRIZE
  Life Is Such A Precious Gift

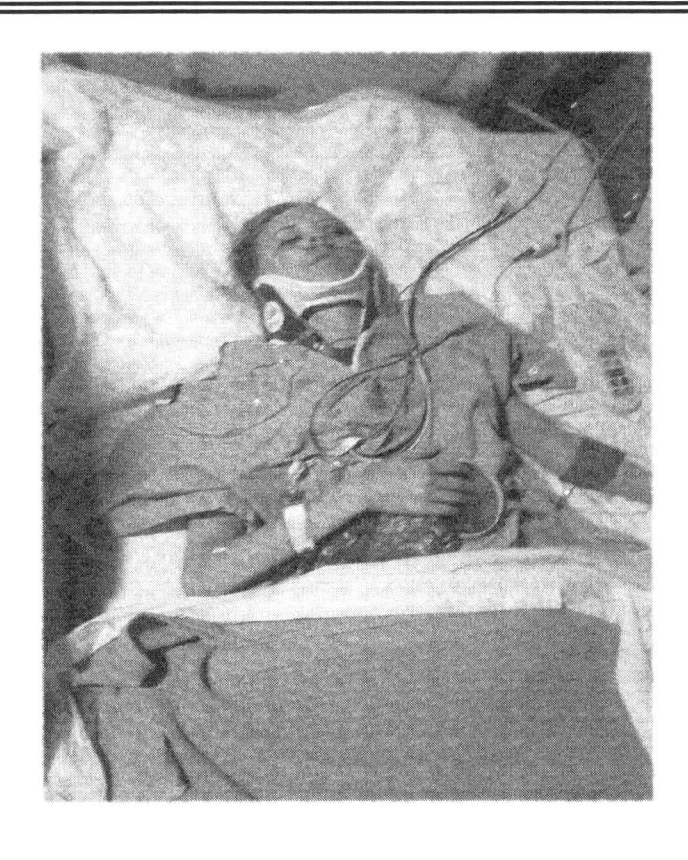

~*Contribution*~

Andi J.

At 29 most of my friends were already married and had started their families. While they were shopping for back to school I was flying to L.A. to work with celebrities. When they were taking trips to the park I was taking trips to Thailand. They drove a minivan and I rode on an elephant.... everything about my life was the polar opposite of theirs and I couldn't imagine ever wanting it to be any different...

It's funny how quickly things can change. I rolled out of bed, at my usual 10 am start time and started to get ready for the day. Since I do promotional modeling I get paid as much in one weekend as I would normally make working a full-time job. I tend to only work about 8 days a month and I loved the freedom it afforded me. I was working a business to business event at the conference center so I had to wear a dress and heels. I quickly got dressed and left for the event. It was a long day but I had fun.

I walked out to my car to drive home but my feet were killing me from wearing heels all day and they were really tall so I was hesitant to drive in them. Luckily I had a pair of sneakers in my car. I put them on.
They looked ridiculous with my nice dress but I didn't care because I was just going to drive home and nobody was going to see me. I was driving along and I remembered that I needed to stop by the client's office to pick up my pay for the day, but I never made it.

I had to get off the freeway on an exit that was under a lot of construction. The ramp was torn up and they had it barreled off so that the exit was extremely short and narrow.

As I started to go for the ramp I hit some gravel and since I was slowing in preparation for the exit it made my car slide a bit toward one of the construction barrels. I didn't know what they were made of (plastic: ok to hit or cement: Will crush you to death) so I swerved to avoid it. For, the record, the barrels are not made of cement so go ahead and hit them if the situation arises. It'll do far less damage than the alternative! Well, swerving on a narrow ramp is obviously a terrible idea, and it had me aimed right at the cement barrier separating the ramp from the freeway. At that point, there was no avoiding it. I knew I was going to crash into something. In my last ditch effort to minimize the impact I tried to hit the brakes and spin my car a bit to avoid hitting the wall head-on.

It all happened really fast but it felt like it was going in slow motion. I spun the car as much as I could as I watched the wall get closer and closer. At the last second before impact I ducked to the side, leaning my body between the gear shift and center console. Then I hit the wall. There was a flash of red and then everything went black.

When I opened my eyes the dust from the airbag was still settling. Thankfully no one else was in my car, I was not on my phone, and no other people were involved. Just me vs a cement barrier and the barrier won! The end of the barrier crunched up the driver side door leaving just a triangle of space that somehow I was lucky enough to get wedged into. Part of the door crunched in and my leg/hip was pinned under it and the seat crunched and squished me too. I was pushed to the side by the crooked seat and the bar that used to make up the door frame.

The airbags were hanging out and had a bit of blood on them. I felt like I was pretty logical in the situation but looking back now I think I underestimated just how hard I hit my head! Instead of freaking out my first thought (after checking to make sure there were no other people involved obviously) was to do an inventory of my car. I just bought new tires, new spark plugs and wires, AND a brand new windshield. I was pretty mad that all the money was going to go to waste but I was very happy to see that my windshield was still in pristine condition. I still had the receipt and fully intended to return it. In my mind that made perfect sense at the time.

I could feel blood running down my face and my head was a little sore so I did a quick mental check on my body. I was having a hard time getting a full breath but I wasn't alarmed because I thought I just knocked the wind out of myself and it would correct itself after a bit. I wiggled my toes first and they moved. I could feel all my body parts and was able to move my hands, arms, head/neck, etc. without problem all except for my knee. It was pinned between the crushed in door and the seat. I thought that I could just wiggle my way out but as I tried to pull my leg out it wouldn't budge. I pulled as hard as I could and I pushed against the door but nothing was working. That's when I started to panic a little bit. I was trapped!

My eyes were watering a bit but my salty tears hurt the cuts on my face so I was trying to stay calm and not cry. All of a sudden in the middle of that panic I felt the most peaceful feeling rush through my body.
I had only ever experienced that one other time in my life and I instantly knew everything was going to be ok. I didn't know how, because I had no savings to my name, I just totaled my only form of transportation, and I was not going to be able to work for a while. By all standards, I had every reason to be panicked.

My life was in complete chaos and yet I felt calm. I quit pushing on the door and as I glanced up I noticed there was a man sitting in my passenger seat. He kind of looked like Hector Elizondo and he was wearing khakis with a long sleeve white shirt and a forest green microfleece vest over top of it. He asked me if I was ok and I told him that I thought I was. Then he asked if I knew who hit me. Instantly I was confused. I started to wonder how long I had really been unconscious because I THOUGHT I had been awake for just about all of it but I didn't remember hitting anybody. A hundred scenarios ran through my head, did someone hit me from behind, did I slide and hit someone else, did I somehow fly over the barrier and cause a massive car pile up for people trying to avoid me?! I was terrified that other people were hurt. I started to panic again.

Did you hit me? I asked him. No, he replied. I let out a sigh of relief. Then I told him, I'm stuck in here and I can't get out. I pushed on the door again and it didn't budge. I could feel my heart starting to race and it was getting harder and harder to breathe. In a very calm voice, he reassured me that I was okay.
The ambulance is on their way he said. I calmed down again. I knew he was right. Help was on the way and they would push the car away from the wall so I could get out and I would be ok. I leaned back on my seat and closed my eyes to try and keep my heart rate down and breathing even.

I never heard the man leave but when I opened my eyes there were firefighters standing on the hood of my car yelling back and forth to each other. They used the jaws of life to cut the entire top off of my car. To my devastation that destroyed the windshield, I was going to replace haha.

After the roof was cut off and peeled back like a giant sardine can a bunch of firemen and EMT's gathered around me. They told me they were going to push a stretcher down in behind my back, strap me to it, and pull me out, which they did. I was really frustrated that I was strapped in because I felt like my breathing would be better if I could just roll onto my side.

Inside the ambulance, they started to cut my dress off but I begged the girl not to because I really liked it. She kindly cut it down the side seam so I could re-sew it. It was a very nice gesture, considering it was covered in blood that would never come out and the back was shredded to pieces. You've really got to appreciate the little details. People can be pretty cool especially when they humor your delusional requests without acting like you're insane. The 2 emt's in the ambulance immediately got to business checking me and they put on a really obnoxious neck brace.

I heard one of them mention pneumothorax which I recognized as a collapsed lung thanks to all the medical dramas I had been watching with grandma. (see, sometimes you learn relevant things from television) I was in good spirits all the way to the hospital and I was cracking jokes the whole time despite the lack of oxygen. I really didn't think things were that bad. When they wheeled me in through the er doors some people gasped and had horrified looks on their faces. That's when I realized I must have looked horrible. I tried my best to look alive and well to show everyone I was ok.

They got me into a room to prep for surgery where one other guy (who was not looking so hot) was also waiting, both of us were still on our stretchers. They finally unstrapped me and I immediately rolled onto my side. A nurse rushed over to me and kept trying to get me to stay on my back but I didn't care. It felt so good to finally breathe! She came back with a few other people and they put one of those annoying tubes in my nose. A doctor or nurse (I'm not sure) came over and looked at my face. He told me he could see the bone so they started stitching....except they forgot to numb it!!! I was kind of wincing with every stitch and part way through he said, "wait, can you feel this?" and I was like "Uh, YEAH!" So they got me numbed up and finished stitching.

At that point, a nurse was trying to get a phone number from me to contact family and I could not for the life of me remember anyone's number except for my childhood friend Matt.

Then a doctor came in and told me I needed to go to surgery to place a tube for my collapsed lung (no surprise there) and that I also needed surgery because I broke my pelvis. Confused I told him that he must be mistaking me for the battered guy in the waiting room because I didn't have a broken pelvis. Thank goodness the car had pinned me in during the accident because I genuinely thought I was fine and I would have tried to walk had I been able to.

While I was waiting to go into surgery my family started to show up. I felt bad because they looked so sad because of me and I felt fine. I wished they had cleaned me up a little before they called my family because I was still covered in blood and glass and banged up and I knew that scared them. I scared one nurse to death when she was taking my blood and accidentally poked herself. She told me it's policy to do an HIV and hep c test after that. I told her that was a good idea because I pierced my bellybutton in an alley, under the stairs, in Thailand. She had me signing consent forms before I even finished my sentence They also decided that would be a good time to do a pregnancy test just for good measure.

Then a police officer came to take my statement. I thought I was fairly coherent, but looking back at my scribble of a signature right across the middle of his statement page I would have to say I was still pretty out of it.
I later looked up the police records for my accident with all the other witness statements. Everything written was as I remembered it EXCEPT, there was no statement from a man and nobody mentions him being there or being in my car.

That leads me to believe he may have been my guardian angel...but I also kinda hope he's not because if he is then I accused him of hitting me when all he was doing was trying to look out for me. If he's my guardian angel the poor guy has already been working overtime as it is! All in all, I cut my face and arm, Lacerated my spleen, broke some ribs, collapsed my lung, broke my scapula and broke my pelvis. It took some stitches, a breathing tube, and pelvic surgery to piece me back together. Our running joke was that even though I broke a bunch of bones it was ok because the blood test had come back negative so I wasn't pregnant.

When I got wheeled to my room after surgery I was still making jokes and trying to show off my single sister's photo to all of the cutest medical staff. I knew my family was scared because they were acting really careful around me like they thought I would break and I could see how scared they were. I was pretty tired so everyone started to leave and mom decided to stay the night with me which was nice of her. During the night I woke up and I was just laying in the dark looking around the room. It was just lit up by the lights from on the monitors and I could hear all the machines beeping and pumping etc. All of a sudden I thought I heard a huge juicy fart! I started to laugh really hard because I thought mom was letting them rip in her sleep. I had to try really hard to control it because every time I laughed it hurt from all the broken ribs.

The next day I realized it wasn't mom making that noise all night it was fluid in the breathing tube so I cracked myself up over my own machine.

[My sister] showed up right after breakfast and offered to help me shower which was really nice. My back was super itchy and I thought it was because of the lack of showering until they went to lift me up into my wheelchair (which would be my new wheels for the next few months) and my entire back was covered in broken glass. I was still sitting on the sheet that had been used in pulling me out of my car so there was still broken glass underneath of me. My sweet sister helped me dig it all out and then helped me wash the blood and glass out of my hair and get cleaned up. I felt more like a person and less like a scary monster after that. Tons of friends and family members came to visit me in the hospital and I feel like that helped me to heal faster.

I was supposed to be in the hospital for a few weeks and then rehab for months but I only ended up being in the hospital for 5 days and then got transferred right away to a brand new rehabilitation facility that was taking on 18 patients for free to get the word out about their facility. As a person with no insurance and a daily shot that cost $100 per shot I greatly appreciated it! I wasn't supposed to use the wheelchair much before I left the hospital but the morning after surgery

 I asked if I could wheel myself around the hall. The dr was hesitant but he told me we could give it a try. I wore myself out but I made it all the way to the end of the hall and back. By the time I went to the rehabilitation center I was wheeling myself most places and showering myself and moving back and forth from my bed to my wheelchair.

Everything seemed to be going great. While I had no job, no car, no savings, and a massive hospital bill, with substantial injuries I still felt optimistic. I didn't know how it would work out but I knew everything was going to be ok. at the rehab facility, we had a fun family game night and I got to visit with more of my friends.

I butted heads with the staff a time or two being my usual stubborn self. Sometimes I refused to go to morning sessions because I was literally SO exhausted! I couldn't figure out why I was so tired but I thought it must just be left over from the accident. I found myself getting overly emotional about things as well. I was easily irritated over small things.

One example is the 4 pm dinner time. I HATED eating that early and was never very hungry at that time. One night I had a particularly rough therapy session and my friends had been kicked out for the night due to visiting hours and the dr was lecturing me because I hadn't gone down to the cafeteria for dinner. "It's a long time until morning and you won't have anything to eat. The kitchen closes at blah blah blah." I tuned him out because I wasn't in the mood for a lecture.

After he left the room I stubbornly grabbed my laptop, googled the nearest Jimmy John's and placed a delivery order. They had my dinner there in under 10 minutes and my doctor just gave an exasperated sigh when he brought it to my room.

It wasn't just irritability either. Sometimes at dinner, I would just start crying for no real reason, but in a place like that nobody questions you if your crying. We are all going through some pretty tough physical stuff to be there in the first place. I cried over Tom and Jerry because they really could have been great friends if they just stopped fighting and one night alone in my room I watched Dumbo and just bawled my eyes out. The way he looked at his mom, and she looked at him just left me with the most hollow, and lonely feeling I had ever experienced in my life.

I cried at night sometimes when I was alone and I cried at every bell ceremony (When people were ready to leave the facility we all went out into the hall and made a long line and clapped for them as they came down the hallway. At the end, right by the door there was a bell and they would ring it before they left to go home) I wasn't sure if I was crying because I was happy for them, or sick of being there, or homesick, or maybe just a mixture of all of it. I cried when a man who had been a bishop took his first steps.

He had been in the facility for a long time and it was putting a big strain on his family. They didn't know if he was going to be able to walk again and the diagnosis had been pretty grim. Then one day while we were all in the therapy room He stood up, holding onto the handrails on both sides of him and without help from anyone he took three steps! He had to sit down after but he did it himself and I remember being so happy for him I just started crying at the table while I finished my exercises. Nobody else at that table had dry eyes either though.

When I talked to my doctor about being so emotional he told me that can happen after a trauma. The lack of a period could be blamed on all the weight I'd lost post accident and stress. The sleeping, stress and rebuilding strength. Every symptom could be explained away by the accident and that's what all the doctors did. I finally left the rehab facility and rang the bell for myself. I was nervous to go home and back to the real world in a wheelchair but I was glad I had a lot of people to help and support me and I coincidentally lived with my grandparents in a house that was wheelchair accessible because of the little boy who had lived there before us. Grandma borrowed a wheelchair from Uncle Chuck.

My neighbor who is also in a wheelchair was really nice to hang out with me and give me tips on how to get around and do things (like laundry). We also got a bunch of supplies, like the shower bench, for free from a non-profit organization in Brigham. Everything was just really falling into place. Then one day something weird happened.
I lost a lot of weight after the accident and I had already been skinny to begin with, so I was trying really hard to gain it back.

Usually this is a big struggle for me but after a while, it seemed to be working. I was gaining weight little by little. So on this sunny morning, I woke up and got some yogurt and a banana like I had done every morning for the past month or so. After eating I headed to the bathroom to attempt a shower but while I was in there I got really sick very suddenly and threw up.

When I came out of the bathroom I told grandma that she shouldn't eat the bananas or yogurt because they gave me food poisoning. It seemed a bit weird since I didn't think yogurt could really go bad, and the banana wasn't mushy, but I brushed it off. Later that day we were having a family barbecue and everyone was over at the house. Grandma had a frozen pineapple and she decided to microwave it to speed up the thawing process. I was clear on the other side of the room but the smell of it instantly made me sick. That's when I knew there had to be a mistake. Lots of things seemed off and people were able to explain it away by blaming it on the accident but you don't develop supersonic smelling powers from a car accident.

I suspected the hospital was wrong about the pregnancy test so I quietly took my sister aside and told her what I thought was going on. She agreed to drive me to the hospital but it was a weekend so I had to go to the urgent care.
She felt really bad leaving me there in my wheelchair to wheel myself in alone but I had no idea what they were going to say or how long it was going to take so I sent her home and went in by myself. I sat and waited for a few hours since it wasn't a huge emergency. I teared up when a boy came in with his mom and dad. He looked terrified but didn't cry.

He was trying to be so brave. I could see they had a towel wrapped around his hand. The dad had a tense jaw and the mom looked like she was fighting back tears. At one point a nurse came out to look at his hand and they had to unwrap it.

I could see his hand was covered in blood and his fingers were in terrible shape. The boy couldn't keep it in anymore. His lip started to tremble and big tears rolled down his cheeks. My heart broke for him. I sat in my wheelchair praying that he would be ok and would feel better soon. His dad gave him the biggest hug and just held him until he stopped crying. I wish I knew what happened to that boy.

They finally came and got me and did a test which came back positive then had me wait in another room until a nurse could come for an ultrasound. It was like, "hey great news you get to be out of the wheelchair soon, but your also pregnant." It felt like it took forever for someone to come tell me what was going on! When the nurse finally came in she asked how far along

I thought I was and I couldn't even tell her. I thought maybe it was a freak symptom of the accident or at most I would see a little blob but when she put the machine on my belly

I saw a FACE!!

He was actually moving around and was easily recognizable as a baby. I heard the heartbeat but it sounded really slow. I thought babies had really fast heartbeats so I asked her if the heartbeat was mine or the baby's and she said it was the baby's. I asked her if it was too slow and if he was ok but she said she couldn't make comments about the ultrasound only a doctor could.

Then she wheeled me back into my room where I spent an excruciating time thinking about all the things that could be wrong to cause a slow heartbeat. Was the baby there during the accident? Was it injured? Could the stress harm or kill it? What about the medication and multiple surgeries and radiation from all the xrays? I tried to prepare myself for bad news. That my baby was hurt or something was developmentally wrong, or worse, not going to make it. When the doctor came in he said he thought things were ok but I needed to check with an obstetrician and with the hospital radiation specialist to figure out what the radiation dosage may have been.

Eventually, the radiologist called me back and told me it should be ok. I got the proper prenatal care that I needed and even though there were a few crazy incidents while I had to sneak around I eventually told all my family and was able to relax a little bit. I worried that I would miscarry or that my baby would be born with 3 eyeballs or severe developmental issues but on a beautiful December day I had a beautiful little boy and he was perfect. He is a sweet, calm baby, and he seems like he was just born knowing how to handle everything. In great chaos, a miracle was born and it righted everything. Since I was pregnant during the car accident the hospital stay for that and for my son's birth were all covered.

The rehab just happened to be accepting new patients for free and I was one of them. The house was wheelchair accessible. I got the supplies I needed....everything about him just has a way of working itself out. He filled that emptiness I had in ways I never knew I wanted or needed. He came here in a whirlwind but it was EXACTLY the way it was all supposed to be.

~MP~
CHAPTER 5

Grandparents are Brilliant!

THEY'VE FOUND A NEW WAY TO HAVE KIDS

ANCIENT PIONEER CONTRIBUTION
GRANDPARENTS ARE BRILLIANT
They've Found a New Way to Have Kids
Gary Reed Burnett

Love in the home-Hope, courage, and determination to keep going and enjoy the journey.

I hope that this perspective will give insight to those of you who may be going through similar circumstances and courage to face whatever challenges lay ahead.

I am the second oldest of my ten siblings and the oldest boy. I have had the opportunity of sharing in the raising of six wonderful children and also have discovered it takes a TRIBE to do so, and now enjoy the great and fun experiences of grandchildren.

**"Grandparents are Brilliant!
They've found a new way to have Kids"
~GB~**

Now consequently, I have an even greater appreciation for my parents for their willingness to sacrifice for our family and their overwhelming perseverance in the face of so much opposition that comes with the territory of having a family, and a very large one at that. I think if you ask my parents they will tell you that the larger number was actually a little easier because they made the comment that the secret sauce was to get the 1st one going in the right direction and then they can show their siblings what to do, and pass it on.

. I am eternally grateful for parents that did not give up

even when at times it must have seemed like their burdens were too much to bare, or the relentless trials and tribulation must have looked insurmountable at times.

Because my parents were willing to persevere and keep going even in the midst of adversity, such as child birth, cloth diapers, diaper pails, poop, poop, and more poop, and then when we are older, we move out and double our problems by adding more individuals to the mix with adult problems instead of kid problems, just to list a few. They have not only changed our diapers, but the very core of who we are. and the lives of our children and their posterity through enduring and loving examples forever. Perfect?...No, but getting closer everyday.

Upon reflection of my childhood I look back with fondness and admiration for the level of commitment and dedication my parents had for each other and for each of their children. I always felt loved and I knew that my parents wanted to provide me with opportunities that would further my abilities and help me grow. I had what I would consider an idyllic childhood. Maybe too good to be true.

At a young age, my parents encouraged us to develop our talents. They provided us with many opportunities such as art, music, and dance and to enhance our skills, and I remember in my very early years learning to work alongside my father and grandfather, and grandmother and mother on construction projects. I have fond memories of our house on Cahoon at the base of the majestic foothills of the Utah Mountains. A reservoir was our neighbor to the east, and on a couple of occasions we got to watch in fascination as our parents tried to fight the floodwaters and soon just had to open the basement door and watch the knee deep fast flowing river run through it. It was really cool! (for us).

When we were little we enjoyed building snowmen with Dad that were taller than him (6') and upon finishing this amazing and magnificent creation I was lifted by my strong father to rest upon this 'magnificent giant and felt as if I was on top of the world.

Dad is a brilliant man (or at least he had us all believing he is because I am about 60 and even knowing all that I know now he still knows so much more in his little pinky. Discussions about anything and everything with Dad is always a treat Expounding on everything is a fun subject because you don't ever have to worry about getting off the subject. You can ramble all you want to, and Oh how we love to ramble. You probably noticed.

Growing up, my parents were conscientious and hardworking and always set high expectations for themselves. They took exceptional effort to make sure that all of us were always up and reading scriptures in the morning and were very tolerant as we came dragging in our pillows and blankets and trying to wipe the sandman out of our eyes with little success. I don't remember much about the scriptures, but I do remember how important my parents thought the daily routine was.

FATHERS

Now that I am a father, I get the importance of consistency. I am awed at the immense effort that was taken to make sure we all had that time together before Dad would have to shuttle out the door to work.. I am certain that for Mom to get ten children out the door all dressed and ready to go for school church or any other activity would have been quite the feat for any parent to achieve.

My parents were always there for us. Just one example of this would be the fishing trip that we took to the Weber River and Dad was in a suit having just put work on hold, but just rolled up his pant legs, grabbed a net, and started scooping out ten pound lunkers at the fish step, because we were not having too much luck as we dangled treble hooks into the falls, but we did get a few and loved fishing.

Or the Family Home Evening, again, he rolls up the suit pant legs, puts on roller skates and he's off and wheeling. Amazingly enough, He would put in a very very long day starting early in the morning scripture study, then off to the military base where he was a top notch Contract Price Analyst, then to work at the (big) family furniture store that my great greats started in the 1800s while Utah was still a territory. My Great Grandfather was a casket maker and as the pioneers stopped dying off he transitioned into fine furniture to the point it was the biggest Union Fleet in the state, and I was running into people that had bought their furniture there in all the four corner states and the west up into Washington as well.

Dad would work late into the night, many times all night and I would go visit him and remember falling asleep under the 190 characters per minute bi-directional console

*printer that was running and spitting out his reports all night and all day long.
I will demonstrate the printer for you.*

Zzzzhhhh zhhhhhhh zzhzhhzh zhhzzzzh zzhz zh zh zhhhzzzt

(it was so advanced it would start back the other way!)

zh zh zhhhzzz zzhz zh zh zhhhzzz zzhz zh zh zhhhzzz ZZZT!

*My father was a hard worker and it was so difficult to try and keep up with him because he was my hero of coarse. I must admit I do not remember meeting anyone in my life that impresses me more than my Dad. Never heard him swear, didn't ever drink, smoke, and always a gentleman to my mother.. Did they ever disagree or argue? Sure, but they had a rule and they shared it with us on their 50th wedding anniversary cruise which we got to go on. Wahoo!
That secret was prayer. It is very difficult to be mad at your spouse, and have a conversation with deity. I struggled with this in latter years because I remember coming home and we were both tired so we said casually,*

"Who's turn is it tonight?

"T think it's yours"

"I'm quite sure it's yours"

"Well let's just say our own private prayers and go to bed"

"Ok"

That's what I remember about the end of a twenty year marriage. I owe my former spouse (I don't think X is very respectful, so we will use former spouse) an apology for not stepping up to the plate and saying couples prayers no matter who's turn it is. I remember thinking it was no big deal at the time.

Mmmmm so what do you think? A mistake? Yep fraid so!

Some things are not in our control no matter how much we wish they were different. That being said, my parents are perfect examples of someone who has been able to learn from their past.

TOMATOES
I remember the story of the tomato and mom was at the store with dad and was having those strange cravings that come during pregnancies, and that moment she felt a huge sensation that she could not live another minute without a tomato.

She picked it up and was salivating, but realized that she did not put this tiny little red delicious gem into the budget, but was thinking,
"Oh, surely I deserve this and it's just this little tomato."
Well it was the middle of winter and the price of tomatoes was WAY HIGH, but Dad just responded,

"You can have that tomato if you really want it, but you are eating the money we are saving for our house. Do you really want that? You're right, it is just a little tomato."

Mom took the tomato out of her cart, pinched her lip and

reluctantly and sadly and longingly placed it back on the shelf.

She still remembers that tomato, but she also remembers sticking to a budget and how wonderful it was to be a home owner. Car owner, and more and more and more because they learned together how to keep a budget together. Did they ever make mistakes?... Yes, but they will tell you that you will come up twice as fast if you make those choices and decisions together as a team.

They taught us about fasting and tithing and how great blessings can come from these.

FASTING

We were very young at the time my grandmother came to the door and announced that our uncle was in a terrible train accident, and the family will be fasting for him.

He was working a rail car on the side track when a moving train unhitched a car while still moving and sent the rail car moving down that track he was on. My uncle was on the roof making repairs and happened to see almost too late the oncoming disaster and tried to jump into the air so that he would be airborne during the crash. Slight miscalculation, and he ended up being smashed between the two and suspended upside down with one leg almost mashed off. Pinned and yelling for help he struggled to stay calm and conscious, but to no avail.

He hung there a very long time passing in and out from loss of blood. They got him to the hospital and the doctor told my Grand Mother and Aunt that he would very likely

need to amputate the leg and there were many problems including gangrene was setting in and it was not looking good.
My grandma was very upset and told him not to cut the leg off, but he interrupted her in saying

"You don't seem to understand. The leg is the last worries. I am not sure he is even going to be with us by morning. We will be operating, so you say your prayers for us too. This is not good. Not good at all. You need to pray for his very life that is hanging in the balance and the gangrene has traveled into the trunk of his body, so please reconcile he may not be with us much longer. He is holding onto dear life."

We fasted and sure enough, My uncle lived. He lived into his 80's and was so fun when we would go water skiing at Pineview reservoir... and man could my uncle slalom!

Years later when he went to work as a security guard and hiss leg was bothering him so he popped it off, and a coworker said" "Hey that's a cool trick. How do you do that?" His coworker never even knew his leg was gone even after knowing him for a long time.
Fasting really works!

TITHING

Because Mom and Dad showed us tithing at a young age it was a snap, and came in real handy when teaching math, and percentages, but was really easy until I got older and had a family and the usual life problems hit the fan. The kind that can test us to the core like Job.

There were massive layoffs, and I was out of work. This was a terrible blow to our young family and we didn't know where to even come up with the money to put food on the table. I was a ward clerk and I realized we were getting behind on tithing and I may not get to be a clerk anymore. I went to the bishop and asked what to do.

He was a kind man, and he gave me the answer that all good bishop's do, and that is I won't tell you what you have to do, but I will share with you that I have seen great blessings come to those that pay their tithing, and shared the scripture that there won't be even enough room to receive it, and then had me visit with my neighbor who was in the bishopric and also a CPA for a profession.

The friend said, "Pay your tithing first and the rest will work out", and proceeded to show me a path to how it could work with a lot of faith.

Because I was a full tithe payer, the bishop was able to help out with the food and to place a food order. That still didn't tale care of the house payment. I was sweating bullets, but when leaving the old job something amazing happened and there was just enough money in a non vested retirement account that was kicked out to me in a lump sum check to take care of the house, the back tithing, and even the food, and I walked into an interview, and got hired immediately, so that we didn't even miss a beat! Not 1 Lick!

The other people from work had the same issues and talked to consumer credit and were advised that you do not have money for charitable contributions, so that's the first thing they cut. It was not so favorable for my coworkers, and I felt bad for them that it did not work out too well.

So at a young age we were expected to work and take care of ourselves. 10 kids and that is a lot of work unless everyone steps up to the plate and takes on the many duties of the household. For heaven's sake, the milk truck delivered 16 gallons of milk 2x a week! Next to the school we were the biggest order on his route. (I drank 2 gallons a week myself)

Some of our weekly responsibilities included taking turns cooking, babysitting, and helping with other various household chores. I'm sure that at the time we begrudgingly completed the tasks and probably would've preferred spending more time playing, but as the older children, we made it possible for everyone to to learn valuable life lessons and have fun while doing it. I loved to do the dishes, as we would have a water fight with the sprayer, and took out 2 birds with one stone because we also cleaned the floors by having to hose down the whole kitchen area. We were able to learn how to work hard, how to be less selfish, how to care for younger siblings, and how to rely on each other, and my siblings are my best friends.

I have always admired the love and respect that my parents have had for one another. My dad has stood faithfully by my mother every step of the way. He has been a wonderful and wise provider, a man of honor and integrity, but the most enduring quality is they both are our best friends, and they love us unconditionally. Sometimes *we stray, make mistakes, or whatever the circumstance may be, or maybe we just have to learn something on our own and they are there to give us support, love and sometimes just that listening ear of a loving parent that helps us know it is going to be okay.*

We will never tire of listening to Dad's stories of the scriptures. My parents continue to persevere in spite of whatever may plague them at this time with age, broken hearts for their children, broken pipes, or you name it, they've seen it. Even though they face many challenges and trials in the process, they continue to teach all the rest of us even more about faith, endurance, and determination.

My parents continue to serve and have undertaken inner city missions, temple service, and more in sharing with others their mortal experiences that sometimes in darkness it helps bring us to understanding, finding and experiencing true happiness and lasting joy.
  Anyone who has been around my parents for long, has unmistakably observed that they are the quintessential essence of hope, light, and love.
They are truly an example of pure love, generosity, and kindness.
Their sacrifice and Love have allowed them to bless the lives of our families, and of many people; and so it is with all of us if we are willing to have hope, courage, and determination to keep on going.

I was watching my parents interact at the hospital on one occasion when my father was in for open heart surgery It was a tender moment and it was something I will not forget during my mortal existence (as long as I keep my faculties anyway)

    Mom: "I love you!"
Dad tried to say"   "I Love you More"
    Mom: "I love you the Most"
Dad: Trying to say "I love you the Mostest

Dad almost ripped the tube out of his throat to top it! My Grandma Neta had a saying as my parents are alive at the time of this writing and think might appreciate it.

"Spread it thick… like honey on bread!
"Don't wait to spread the BULL"
    "Til After I'm DEAD!"
        `~*Grandma Neta*~

We can start spreading now that we've shared the facts!

Grandma Neta's little sayings:

1- You are not a darn site better than I am to work
2- Choose Wisely because your decisions are brief but endless
3- You may fly around the roses but you could land in the manure
4- A job worth doing is a job well done
5- Where there is a will there is a way\
6- Fix it up...Clean it up...Wear it out...or do Without
7- Take Freedom away and what do you have...Mere Animals
8- No deal is a good deal if you can't afford it
9- If you are going to do the job, do it right or don't do it at all
(My Saying: Anything worth doing is worth doing again)
10- If a dog bites you once... it's his fault, dog bites you twice it's your fault
11- Worrying is like a rocking chair...back and forth back and forth but gets you nowhere
12- Many Hands make light work
13- Many a slip between the cup and the lip
14- If you don't like my gate, don't swing on it
15- The size of a man's nest egg depends on the chick he picks
16- A person convinced against their will is of the same opinion still

~MP~
CHAPTER 6

**HEALING: The other side of the veil
Nora Burnett**

~Contribution~
Nora Burnett

My son passed away at the age of 26. He ended his life after suffering with severe mental illness. He had been diagnosed with many mental and physical debilitating disorders: bi-polar, severe depression, extreme anxiety, borderline personality, ehlers danlos syndrome, paranoia, psychotic, Asperger's, schizophrenic and fiber myalgia. He also experienced opioid addiction. Towards the end of his life, he was in so much mental anguish and physical pain, there was no Doctor, Therapy, Psychiatrist, ECT treatment or ER that could ease his torment.

Now in hindsight, I can finally see this to be true, even after going over it in my head a million times as to what I could have done to change the outcome, as his Mother and caregiver. On a day to day basis, my husband and I would never know what each day would bring. We loved our son and tried desperately to be good caregivers. It seemed we were constantly fighting an uphill battle that could never be won.

Many times, my son would beg us for our help, and we would try to do all we could, then we would start to feel manipulated and then feel guilty for not meeting the endless needs of the "black hole" he felt inside, a black hole that could never be filled to what truly plagued him. Then there were the times we would back off, realizing we were trying too hard to rescue him and creating more problems. We wanted him to be self-reliant and safe and not depending on us for the rest of his life. With his mental and physical disabilities, we tried to teach him the skills and tools he would need to help him function on his own. Then often times it seemed his situation would go from bad to worse and we would step in and continue the cycle of rescuing.

As a caregiver, one of the hardest things for me was to watch my son suffer through the decisions he made or wouldn't make because of his disabling illness. If there was anything I could do to help, I would try to do it, but I had to learn the hard way that there is a fine line between healthy care giving and rescuing. Rescuing can be enabling. I have since learned that rescuing can often take away a person's agency to act for him or herself for opportunity to grow.

There were also those times when my spouse and I were not on the same page as to what would be best for our son and that usually led to marital stress and division and created a negative effect on the whole family including his other three siblings.

There were hopeful times, times when we would start to see the light at the end of the tunnel. Seeing our sweet, fun loving son start to take hold of his true potential and accomplish his goals; for he was very gifted. We wanted so much for him to be happy. I am so grateful for the good times we shared and I will always hold them dear in my heart.

Being a caregiver, I always did better when I was getting enough sleep and eating well, which I honestly did not do all the time, sometimes I let stress get the better of me. When I did take better care of myself, there was more of me to go around, and I could handle life a lot better and I might add, a little chocolate can go a long way too! Writing a daily journal or log for my son was always helpful. I could go back to a certain day and see how he was doing behavioral wise or what medication might be affecting him. It helped a lot. There were times I needed "just me time" or time to get away with my husband or sisters. It made all the difference in the world!

In closing my contribution to this amazing and healing book, I would tell you (the reader) never give-up for the person you are care giving for. Even though my son is not here, I know his spirit has moved on. I am a Christian and I know that this world is not the end. I know I will see my son again and that brings a great deal of comfort and Joy to my soul. I know he is working on things there that he wasn't able to do here.

~MP~
CHAPTER 7

SAVE save SAVE!
When 1 and ½ bushels = 90 bushels

Record of Keziah Miles Goodman Warner Maw and retold by Great, Great Great Great Grandson-From Her Bible journal

I, Keziah Miles Goodman Warner Maw, was born on May 2, 1834 in Hallaton, Leicestershire, England. I joined the Church of Jesus Christ of latter-day Saints and was baptized March 4, 1854 in England.

I left England, November 22, 1854 on the ship," Clara Wheeler." After we had been at sea for a day and a half a terrible gale came up, and the captain signaled for a pilot and he took us back to the port where we had to wait several days. However we were not allowed to leave the boat. During our stay, there were 21 couples married on board ship and I was one. I was married to brother William Warner of Glooston, England. We held a fast day and prayed and the Lord did stop the storm and the Saints again started out. It took us six weeks after leaving Liverpool, England to reach New Orleans.

The next day after arriving in New Orleans. We took a riverboat up the Mississippi River to St. Louis. It was very cold and they were cutting the ice on the river. We spent Christmas day on board the boat.

On January 17, 1855. We reached St. Louis and then had winter for sure. I and the women stayed there until the following April, when brother Warner and brother Miles Andrews with others went up the country to get work. Later I went up the Missouri River, where some of the sisters to Atchessions camp. There, with many others, I took the cholera and was very sick for a long time. Many who took it died. One of the brothers sent for brother Warner and he cared for me until I was well again after I recovered. He went to work on the farm. There until 25 July, then we restarted with ox teams to cross the plains.

We were the last company of the season to cross the plains. There were 50 or 60 wagon loads are oxen were very wild one day an Indian came up with his bright colored blanket and frightened the first team. This started, all of them running and stampeding. A boy fell out of the wagon and was killed.

During our travels. Many took sick and died, and we had to bury them by the roadside, many of the oxen died also, and we were forced to leave some of the wagons behind. Before we arrived at our destination. Our supplies ran low, but Brigham Young, who was expecting us, for out manned and provisions to meet us

We arrived in the Salt Lake Valley, November 1, 1885. I had to remain in Salt Lake for three weeks, while brother Warner and others went back to get the wagons we had to leave behind. By this time, winter was drawing near, and the grasshoppers had eaten up most of the crops, so provisions were very scarce and hard to get. But brother Brigham Young for us and brother and sister Stolworthy on the church farm up to cache Valley, which is between Logan and Mendon. Sister Stolworthy and I were the first white women living in the cache Valley. Sister Stolworthy had the first white child born in cache Valley, which was a girl. If I had remained there three weeks longer, my eldest boy would have been the first white boy child born there.

There were lots of Indians and squaws there and just us two white women and seven men. All the others took cattle and horses down the river bottoms for winter. Pres. Young told us to be very kind to the Indians and feed them or else they would kill us. This we did till we had almost nothing for ourselves. We only had very little wheat left and were snowed in the Valley with no cattle or horses. We used to grind the wheat in the little coffee and make gruel out of it to make it last longer.

After our wheat was gone, we didn't know what to do so one young man named John Dowdle said he was going to settlement for supplies or die in the attempt. He had to cross the mountains and the country all on foot, which was very dangerous for wolves and wild Indians alone. The friendly Indians told him not to go or he would surely die, but he would die anyway, so with our faith and prayers, He started out.

He arrived all right for the Lord blessed him in a few days, he returned on a mule with a sack of flour. It was a long [dangerous] trip for one sack of flour to be divided among so many, but it was the sweetest and best flour any of us had ever tasted. He had many wounds on his legs, were wolves had attacked him. As soon as possible Brigham Young sent us more flour. We were rationed to 1 pound for each man, and 1/2 pound for each of us women. We had nothing else, no butter, milk, or vegetables, but plenty of beautiful water, for which we were very thankful for. Out of many little share, I used to save one full cup full of flour a week.

Brother Warner, and I left cache Valley for Ogden on 22 July. Up to this time I had saved 23 pounds of flour out of our share. Had I not done this. I should have had a bit when my first baby was born three weeks later, on August 4. We arrived in Ogden. By this time.
My husband works with brother Robson and received 20 acres of land and payment down in the forks of the Weaver River. It was covered with willows and trees which she had to grub off. That fall on a 5 acre field where the Union Depot now stands he and brother Robson gleaned wheat from which he had got one and 1/2 bushels of wheat. Then he cleared 2 acres of our own ground and plant that that one and 1/2 bushels of wheat. At harvest time. He got 90 bushels in return.

The next wall. My husband had to go to Echo Canyon to meet the Johnson's Army, who were coming to kill the Mormons. He carried his rifle, but he had no bullets. I, with my baby, was left in the little willow and he had built for a house.

Brother Warner had made the adobes and put up the walls of our little house, but hadn't gotten the roof on when the bugle called and he had to leave. Bishop Erastus being him for a man to put the roof on my house he put willows a mentor without windows or floors and moved in. Then there came a big rain and all the mud began to come through on my bed, so I got up and put the table slanting over the bed, then sat with the baby in my arms until morning under the table. The next day brother, Samuel Bert came and took me to his home
. Then he went and scraped the mud off my floors and fixed the roof again. I went back and stayed there till my husband came home. While my husband was away, brother Robson thrashed and cut our 2 acres of grain and we got 90 bushels of wheat out of one and one half planted. Then brother Warner came home from Echo Canyon and just got our ground plowed ready for the next planting when the heat came from Pres. Brigham Young – – – not to plant, but to get ready to move south. The army was going to pass through and brother young didn't think it would be safe, so he helped them back to we all moved south so our land had to be left unplanted

On the ninth day of April, we arrived in Salt Lake City. There, one of the brothers was leaving, so we took his home on the 11th my second baby was born while we stayed there, six other babies were born there was no doctor, a midwife care for all of our babies. From there we traveled to Summit, Sanpete County, and stayed there till 19 July and then came back to Ogden to our little house which we sure thought a lot of even if it didn't have any windows or floors

The first thing my husband did was to look at his farm and to his surprise he found a lovely patch of wheat nearly ready for harvest, which amounted to 56 bushels. This made 146, Bush bushels of wheat grown on 2 acres from 1 1/2 bushels planted. We surely felt blessed by the Lord. Brother Robson and family stayed for two or three years and we realized the good of all the grain. When he returned, brother Warner made it right with him.

Time passed until 1863, when my husband, brother Warner was working on the Ogden branch canal and a big cave of earth buried him to the waist with two other men (they were buried all over). Brother Warner wouldn't allow his fellow workmen to dig him out until they [tried to help] the other man out, who were buried all over. He stood the weight and the pressure of the dirt under his body so long that he was badly crushed internally and the doctor only gave him five days to [live]. But he lived 14 days. The other men lived many years after.

.Brother Warner died on Sunday morning, and as the crops had to be taking care of. They all got to work and made his [took care of his crops], and then closed that day and buried him and moonlight Sunday night. There was no embalming those days.

We were married on the scene and he was buried by moonlight. He was the fourth person buried in the Ogden city Cemetery. I was left a widow was poor little children, no relations in the country and a large farm.

After a time, brother, Charles Welch brought brother Maw (Edward) from plain city, Utah to visit with me and we became very good friends, and were soon married. He had a small girl about four years old named Alice, which I raised with my children. We live together about 30 years and six more children. When brother, Maw, to, was called by God on August 9, 1893. I was left alone again, but by this time my family was getting large, and the Lord blessed me and was with me at all times.(Signed) Keziah Goodman Warner Maw

~MP~
CHAPTER 8

DIRT-All families have it!

~Contribution-M Burnett

Dirt, all families have it!

I was fortunate and grew up in the perfect family! Loving parents, food and lots of dirt to play in and around.

As a young boy, I loved to be out and doing things. Didn't really matter if others called chores work or play. For me, everything outside seemed like play and everything inside the home seemed like work. Unfortunately, to those who wanted me to do chores around the house, it was their chore to convince me to work. Growing up I found conflict as a way to get out of housework. I think I had this weird idea where no one was going to pressure me into doing something I didn't want to do. It held fairly true growing up. I had brothers that beat on me to get me to mow the lawn and parents that unsuccessfully tried discipline techniques. I just would not bend to others.

My mother spanked me and I laughed at her in a mocking tone about how little it actually hurt. She gave up spanking me when she broke a hairbrush on my backside and after the use of a hanger didn't slow my mouth. I deserved a belt, but she never tried that.

My parents went to a teacher parent conferences and were told about how good of a kid I was. I had a teacher that lavished praise on me as I stayed after school in Jr. High to play chess with him. My parents wondered why I was so hard to discipline at home and such an angel everywhere else.

I had nine siblings and as an adult I know the house work required my hands to work as much as anyone else. One Saturday my mother had asked me to clear the kitchen floor after I refused to do anything else, like vacuum. Kind of odd to think she somehow felt giving me a harder job would encourage me to work. It didn't and I quickly let her know I was not going to do any of it. She tried grounding me and other threating tones to get me to engage in some work. I told her nope and used my mocking tone to let her know she couldn't change my mind.

This particular Saturday she had a new approach to try. After some of the usual methods of encouragement she brought my grandma "Neda", my Dad's mother, into the discussion. She thought she would have some power of persuasion with me. I was known as grandma's "peanut", as I was affectionately called. I had enjoyed being around the ankles of my grandparents during the construction of several houses. My mother had been secretly discussing the difficulty in raising me knowing I loved to do work with her. Why – because the work always building something and usually out of the house

Just mentioning her didn't get me working so my mom picked up the phone and my grandmother came over immediately. As she began to talk to me, I used the mocking language I had used with my mother. My attitude shocked her and my determination not to do any housework. She began to cry!

It was wrong to avoid housework and I knew it. It was even bigger to reject the concern my grandmother had in being there.

What I didn't see clearly at the time was just how my actions affected others. Her last ditch was to entreat me with her homemade apply pie if I would do the work. I refused and she left for home crying and letting me know she cared about me and was disappointed. She also said, "The offer of a fresh baked apple pie stands if you change your mind".

My prior feelings were such that I was in charge of myself. Nobody could force me into anything. When it came to chores that got left undone, so what! But the tears weighted me down with an emotion I didn't like. After everyone gave up on me doing the chores, I got the bucket of soap and scrubbed the entire floor by hand. I thought I had made a valid point about not being forced into anything.

Years later I learned my grandma had a young extended family member who needed some parenting stay with her. Over time and consideration her and husband (Omer) decided they could not permanently adopt this individual who needed some parenting. She left their home after some struggles with disciplining her. The rest of this girls' life was not easy and she passed away in sorrows. My grandma let me know that not trying to do more for this individual was a big regret. When I learned about this story from my grandma I recognized what I had seen in her as she appealed to me to clean the floor. She cared! There were other emotions too, but no doubt she cared enough to have regret about her abilities to help someone else see things with a better perspective. A perspective that would allow for peaceful living.

My grandpa Omer was physically a strong man! Possibly the strongest I have ever known and even in his older age was an astonishment. He was also thought of by many as, "a gentle giant". His hands were strong, with wrists that were as wide as the average man's arm. He had worked for the gas company as a ditch digger. He dug ditches for piping using an old spade shovel and he had developed a talent to dig fast! At around 14 years old my grandma had taken me and a friend to work on a home to be remodeled. It needed a side porch entrance area changed to allow basement entrance without flooding.

It required a four to five foot dig downward into the soil. To accomplish anything while digging, we had to toss the dirt up over the embankment of dirt created by the digging. This was no small detail as the mound quickly exceeded our height as 14-16 year olds.

During the dig my grandpa had gotten the friend and I into a competition to see who could dig out a section of dirt the fastest. We aggressively shoveled and were so quick that much of what we threw up on the embankment came back down at us. Dirt also rolled back and over into where my grandfather was digging. I never heard a whisper of complaint from him as he encouraged us in this digging race to see who would be the best.

So here is what I remember about that day. My grandpa dug faster and more dirt than both of us could as an old man. He did it without complaint and encouraged us both to be the best we could be. Both I and the friend wanted to win. We wanted to win so badly that we dug fast but without thought or planning. I am certain my grandfather saw and felt our short comings as our dirt often tumbled back at him that we failed to fully throw over the embankment.

Funny thing was, he moved more dirt in less time than the both of us combined and still praised us like we were doing all the work. We knew what was happening and that was fun work!

I learned a valuable lesson from these two grandparents in their own ways of teaching. All of us in families or as groups have some dirt that spills back into the lives of others around us. In a quiet moment of reflection about caring for others I ask,

1 Have I shied away from needed work because what we know doesn't fit with who we think we are?

2 Have I been discouraging others with thoughts surrounding hardships and a desire for moral correctness?

Well I have seen the impossible happen! Youthful ignorance gave way to charitable reason.

Now I know that entreating with tears of concern and fostering encouragement with the dirt falling back upon me is often a lifting for others. I know because I have watched a young boy as stubborn as any mule move on their own to work. I scrubbed a floor and ate a homemade apple pie. I dug a ditch and felt validated for good work. Working not for the desire of winning, but in the caring and longer lasting prize of accomplishment.

Maybe the most important lesson, don't let the dirt falling into your life from ever rising embankments stop the work of building something with others. Share in a trial, stop worrying if you have a heavier shovel than the person next to you and get to an accomplishment! That's what those whom you love and work really want anyway. I can still taste the memory of that apple pie!

They hit the newspaper as their faithful testimonies created a stir and was noticed. If a young missionary was homesick they were sent to my grandparents for a meal of homemade fruit canned by them, nurtured, and put to work cleaning the bathroom. This worked in almost every case. Work and laughter was the best medicine and Grandma had many sayings with one famous one being,

"Many hands make light work!"

Grandpa Pete was quite the inventor and it was a joy to see him create with wood things such as a footstool with storage. Many hours went into his towel bar and niterider inventions. (for reading with a light) At Boyle's furniture I got to work side by side with both my grandparents. Loyal customers would ask for Pete Boyle because they knew they were working with a man of integrity. He was a skinny spitfire with a sure testimony of the gospel that he was unafraid to share. Grandma Margie was infamous for her Sunday dinners and we would hang out by the phone praying that we would be the lucky family to feast at her table. Not only did she feed faces the soul was nourished as well. Many a conversation was had as we ate a delicious meal and strong ties were made with these treasured memories. Family Scriptures in the mornings and Family Nights with a talent show were big. Many a time we were uncooperative yet taking note just the same. There was great love in the home and whatever disagreements my parents had were resolved behind closed doors. My Mom would say,

"Use language of intelligence." This meant no swearing.

Who can say they never saw their parents swear or fight. This love carried me through some really tough times. Each of us have a cross to carry and one of mine has been a mental illness diagnosis-bipolar which manifested in my adult years after having children. The gift of my large family blessed me as they rotated and took turns watching over me. Over the years with medical advancements and as I have learned to be diligent with self care and seek professional help I am living a rich full life. The book I got to be the author of is

Illuminating Love In the Home-Spotlight on Mental Illness.

This was inspired by the light, hope and great faith that has been exemplified by my parents and siblings and the book shared with others who are suffering in this way with tips for caregivers too.

Let it be known that there is light at the end of the dark tunnels of our mortal existence and through the healing Atonement of Christ joy can be chosen in this life!

~MP~
CHAPTER 10

A FEW THINGS TO SAY ABOUT MOTHERS

& More

Contribution-A few words to Say: Grandma Vaneta (Neta) Burnett

MOTHERS

I would like to say a few things about Mothers and wives, mothers of our children.

From some point of view Mother's Day has more important events in our lives than another other day except Sunday. Our Mothers and wives have had more influence in determining the quality of our lives than anyone else and should therefore stand next to God in our affection and appreciation and honor we show. Napoleon was once asked what was the greatest need of France and he answered, "Good mothers. Let France have good Mothers and she will have good sons." By the act of thinking about, caring and honoring our Mothers, we lift ourselves up.

In President David O. McKay's great book, Gospel Ideals, he wrote…"Last night I dreamed about my Mother," and then he said, "I would like to dream of my Mother more often and relive those wonderful days I spent at my Mother's knee while I was learning from her the lessons of life that brought me to my present station. They were the lessons of honor, truth and godliness.

Our lives can be greatly benefited by remembering our Mother's trials and sacrifices for us. Whatever may have been said about the sins of the fathers, it has also been said the virtues of the fathers shall be visited upon the children. Thirty-four hundred years ago out of the lightening and thunder of Siani, God said, "Honor thy Father and Mother."

The Prophets have pointed out that the family must be perfected together. Parents cannot receive their greatest eternal glory without the children. Mothers cannot receive their greatest happiness either here or hereafter unless we as sons and daughters live godly upright lives

God has given us a plan. It was He who organized the family in the first place and told us if we would live right, the family could maintain its identity and unity throughout eternity. Certainly God was not thinking only of a few years when He said it was not good for man to live alone, and he set up in each of our homes a Mother to perform a special service for us on this earth. As we look upon her with love and honor, we tend to make her ideals and ambitions ours and we tend to establish a place in our lives for her. Our Mothers, whose body nourished us, whose loving arms sustained us, whose every thought was to help us to do and become what we should be.

She is our wisest counselor, our most effective teacher, our most faithful supporter, our best friend, our Mother. Abraham Lincoln may well have been representing us when he said," All I am or ever hope to be I owe to my angel mother." I would like to read a poem.

The words that came to each child from the heart of his Mother.

Do you know that your soul is of my soul a part
That you seem to be filler and core of my heart.
None other can please me as you, dear, can do.
None other can please or grieve me as you.
Remember the world will be quick with it's blame.
If sorrow and shame ever darkens and covers your name,
Like Mother, like son is the saying so true.
The world will judge largely of Mother by you.
Be yours then the task as the task it must be
To force the proud world to pay homage to me.

Be sure it will say, when the verdict is won,
Be she ever so proud how this man is her son.
Talk about children.....
Every effort must be made to wisely direct children that they may be fortified to live well in this topsey, turvey world.

David O. McKay once said, "Mother in her office holds the keys of the soul and she it is who stamps the coin of character."

The older I grow, the more grateful I am for the life and influence of my Mother. Not just today but in past years. Mothers have always needed the patience of Job, the simplicity of Simple Simon and a sense if ginir to rear children.

Then I am reminded of the Savior when hung on the cross with his throat parched with vinegar looking down at his grief stricken Mother at the foot of the cross and at John his beloved disciple, He said, "Woman, behold thy son. John, behold thy Mother."

The mothers of today must realize that instinct does not furnish all the equipment necessary to meet her child's rearing problems and Mother's love is not an adequate substitute for knowledge and efficiency. She must make a scientific approach to her task of child guidance. She must recognize that divine wisdom must constantly be applied in solving her problems. She must wisely appraise her situation and earnestly try to preserve fundamental values.

Motherhood in Retrospect

What we make of motherhood in life depends on ourselves. The same skies that are dark to one may be glorious and blue to another. Many times in trying to grasp the material things beyond our reach, we leave unseen and unappreciated the many sweet bits of happiness that lie close to us.

I look at these young mothers and I know that their task is not easy. Though children bring their compensations and joys, looking back I know every mother experiences moments of sorrow, days of anxiety and great sacrifice and most of all great responsibilities. But as I look at these young mothers, I know they can and will meet the challenge.

Today Mother finds herself living in a world of confusion. She faces a streamlined speeded up world. The pattern of my youth was not the pattern of children and mothers today. My pleasures were found mostly in the home and small community and ward with a more even tempo.

Today my children and grandchildren are in high powered cars. They mingle with girls and boys who smoke and use alcoholic beverages that in my day would have made especially a girl a social outcast. Today these things are socially accepted by many people.

Economic problems today are pronounced. Living standards are growing increasingly high and human wants are astronomical. The simple things that brought joy to me would scarcely thrill the girl of today. The problems of bridging the gap between Mother and children, the task of meeting the economic needs , the difficulties in rearing a family in an atmosphere of kindness and affection in today's world are overwhelming. But I know you young mothers will be successful and merit the praise of the nation on Mother's Day and the respect and gratitude of those children whose lives you are molding.

We know the family unit is an eternal thing and family ties are sacred.

One of the greatest privileges which God in His kindness has granted us is that of bearing children, of mothering the spirits He created and has allowed to come here. But with this privilege came the responsibility of guiding these spirits into happy, useful lives, worthy of going back into the family circle of the heavenly home when life is done.

A Parent's Prayer

O Master, make me a better parent. Teach me to understand my children, to listen patiently to what they have to say, and to answer all their questions kindly. Keep me from interrupting them and contradicting them. Make me as courteous to them as I would have them be to me. Give me the courage to confess my sins against my children and to ask their forgiveness when I know I have done them wrong.

May I not vainly hurt the feelings of my children. Forbid that I should laugh at their mistakes or resort to shame and ridicule as punishment. Let me not tempt my children to lie or steal. So guide me hour by hour that I may demonstrate by all I say and do that honesty produces happiness. Reduce, I pray, the meanness in me. May I cease to nag and when I am out of sorts, help me to hold my tongue. Blind me to the little errors of my children and help me to see the good things that they do. Give me a ready word for honest praise. Help me to grow up with my children, to treat them as I would those of their own age, but let me not expect of them the judgment and convention of adults. Allow me not to rob them of the opportunity to wait upon themselves to think, to choose and to make decisions. Forbid that I should ever punish them for my own self satisfaction. May I grant them all their wishes that are reasonable and my I have this courage to withhold

A privilege which I know will do them harm.

Make me so fair and just, so considerate and companionable to my children that they will have a genuine esteem for me. Fit me to be loved and imitated. With all Thy gifts, of great Master, give me calm, poise, and self-control. Amen.

Grandmothers

Life smiles as we advance in years and become grandmothers. Bryant Hinkley wrote, "Children interest me, challenge and fascinate me as nothing else can. My own children are boys and girls grown up and gone to their own homes. That's what makes grandmothers. But I thank the Lord for the shouts and laughter of grandchildren. Honest and industrious children are our most precious possessions. The future waits upon them, In their hands is the future, destiny of the world."

Allen Beck gives us the definition of a boy. I like it. "Boys come in all assorted sizes, weights and colors. Mothers and grandmothers love them. Little sisters hate them, big sisters and brothers tolerate them, but heaven protects them.

A boy is truth with a dirty face, beauty with soiled fingers, wisdom with bubble gum in its hair, and the hope of the whole future with a frog in its pocket. But he is grandmothers and mothers captor, jailor, your boss and your master, a freckled face, pint size, cat chasing bundle of noise.

But when you are home alone at night with only the shattered pieces of your hope and dreams, he can mend them with just one word, Hi."

Adversities when met triumphantly can breed in our children and grandchildren patience, industry and consideration for others. There is no Royal Road to achievement, no easy process for building character in our children and grandchildren. We need not seek it. It cannot be found easily but what do we get for nothing.
Nothing with a capital N.
Someone has said character is a hardy plant that thrives best where the north winds blow and is tempered with the sunshine. Great souls have come up through tribulation and not from sheltered ease.
It is the things we overcome that make us strong. That's the reason the Lord made the world hard. We do most for our children and grandchildren when we help them to help themselves, to become reliant, to make good decisions, to formulate plans and to walk alone secure and unafraid.
I want the world to love my children and grandchildren. I will always love them no matter what they do. I may not love what they do but I will still love them. But the world will only love them if they conduct their lives in a Christ-like manner. We grow old, years wrinkle the skin but to give up enthusiasm wrinkles the soul.
The only way we can avoid old age is to die.
There is nothing more refreshing than to have your children and grandchildren come dashing in to say "Hi." All people want to be recognized. They want respect and consideration shown them. No one has the power to hurt you or to elevate you as your children and grandchildren. I would like to say if we would be happy, we make our home a center of hospitality. That is what being a grandmother means to me. I am only as happy as my unhappiest grandchild.
From George Q. Cannon, September 1, 1899, Juvenile Instructor

Extravagance is the sin and peril of the age. Either from the example of others, or the laxity of their own principles, people are prone to live beyond their means. What ever they earn they spend more. Debt is easy to fall into, but its slavery is terrible. It discourages ambition. It is a drag upon high endeavor. It is slow but consuming death to an honest and sensitive soul. War hath slain its thousands but debt its tens of thousands. It makes of him whom it catches in its toils a serf and either a coward or a scamp. It grows like canker, it burns like caustic, it grinds on and on till the grave closes over its unhappy victim. It eats relentlessly any of his substance not only while the world is awake and active, but also while all the world sleeps. No lock or bar can keep out its blight. In no clime or concealment can the debtor escape it clutches. To earn a little and spend a little less means contentment.

Courage in facing one's fellows incentive, to bravely struggle with the world's adversities and honor and reputation of the most priceless sort. Peace of mind is a jewel beyond compare. Whether it be associated with wealth or poverty or be found in that genial middle zone where contentment with a little holds sway. But debt is a tormentor and a mill stone about the neck and is the natural and sworn enemy of happiness. Shun it, reader, as [you] would a serpent.

***

Transcribed from her Standard Examiner Clipping]
A Letter to the Editor- Ogden Standard Examiner-

Class Suggestion

Editor, Standard Examiner:

    Regarding the recent controversy on sex education in our city schools, I feel that first of all, the "name-calling" could be eliminated. Second, if all persons concerned with the subject would read the article in the Nov. 15, 1966, issue of Look magazine entitled "Sweden's New Battle Over Sex," it will tell what 10 years of sex education have taught such things as abortion, contraceptive uses, venereal disease, etc. By high school age, student[s] regard pre-marital relations as natural and acceptable. Contraceptives can be purchased by anyone from automatic vending machines available at all hours. However, some of the kids are not motivated to prevent pregnancy nor VD. Today Swedish experts are baffled by the increase in unwanted pregnancies and VD. The program is now being re-examined.

  ---Certainly we should avoid Sweden's mistakes. Let us hope the sex education program is not a fad such as the cigarette one and find 10, 20 or 30 years later that it was all a mistake.

  ---Some program is in line and could be taught in hygiene course would definitely be more but the impact of an intensive course woul [would] definitely be more harmful than helpful.

  ---And most certainly parents should have the privilege of deciding to what extent the program should be carried out for their sons and/or daughters

    V. Burnett

~MP~
CHAPTER 11

THE ROCKET ROOST

A Nephew's Recollection

Aunt Pauline was a wonderful person and had a beautiful smile. When the cousin's would visit our house for breakfast they always said homemade pancake syrup was better. When I was seven three of my siblings and I tried to run away and our confidant was Sandra her daughter. We became cold and tired and tried to hide in Pauline's basement pantry. Sandra had multiple helpings for dinner and Pauline became suspicious that something was up so We were told to leave the house and hide in the backyard and allow Dan age 4 to find us. He found us hiding in the "Rocket".

Pauline brought us in the home and made sure we were safe and then called our parents and sent us home. Pauline's home in her latter years was directly behind my parents home. My parents and her would have many meals together and would check up on each other daily. Pauline made special effort to attend my children's musical recitals and events. She would bring fancy cupcakes to our Memorial Day bar-b-cue's. We enjoyed being invited to dinner in her home and were amazed at good the food was. She had a wall in the dining room with a tribute to her family members who served in the military. Dan the one who found us hiding being the crown jewel, Colonel Burnett. She was a wonderful aunt and I was great full to know her.

Dave. B.

I was also her attending eye care doctor and she was a model patient.

~MP~
CHAPTER 12

LOVE AT HOME
G. Roai Burnett

MODERN PIONEER CONTRIBUTION
LOVE AT HOME

Gary Reed Burnett

Mother

I have observed how Heavenly Father is quite reserved with what He shares about our Heavenly Mother.. I am reluctant in expressing these thoughts and emotions , but feel they do need to be said to my wonderful mother.

On the cover of my book is a small little hand claspping hold of his mother's hand. I beleive I remember being that little baby in your arms and the cute sweet soft noises and whispers you would make in my ears that would put a smile on my little newborn face ...and no it was not GAS! (Well okay, maybe it was, but a little of both.

Because of your loving embrace the security and love that I was able to have growing up was almost unreal. I felt so comfortable and loved in this world, it was very pleasant and I had a very easy going disposition. Now as I am in the world, I realize what a gift that was, and also how richly blessed I was to the point I was almost not ready to handle such a punishing and mean world.

When I left home I did fell armed with a knowledge and testifmony of a living Savior that you and Dad helped me attain at a very young age of 12 years old.

I recieved that beautiful Book of Mormon with the gold leafing around the pages, and after a week of intense reading, I could not put it down. Tears flowed from my eyes as Alma was forced to watched his loved ones burn at the hands of evil men. Nephi, and the struggle with his siblings, moving, and of coarse inspiring me to live in a tent for consecutive 40 days and 40 nights, and 100 days in a year not too long ago to see how it feels. And by the way, it was really nice. Probably way nicer than what they had to deal with. Neverthelss, a new and wonderful adventure.

I was able to find out that it does not matter where you live, but how you live. I was able to enjoy homes through my life, and was greatful for them, but I was just as grateful for the canvas roof as well. Just different materials, but all were welcomed and it was wonderful that you were able to teach us the difference between a house and home, and thank you Dad for providing Mom the necessary abundance for her to build and create and turn a house into a home.

I also appreciate that you shared the story of our friends coming over to play at our house because their mother was so maticulous that she would not let them play in her imaculate home. In later years her kids grew up and didn't come around much, and she was so lonely, but her house was microscopic clean.

Thank you for sharing that we want to have our home so clean that we could invite the Savior in, but not so clean it chases the spirit away, and thank you for the quiet room. A place that was always ready for guests, or we could go to have quiet reverent time to think or ponder.

Love at Home, A wonderful song that we enjoyed and sang at the church roadshow, and I still remember the new plaid flare legged bell bottom pants you got us (Cant wait for that to come back in style again...NOT!)

.Music and art filled the room along with babies, babies, and more babies. I enjoyed every new addition. Some may think I didn't enjoy maybe a sister or so, but they would be wrong. I enjoyed all of my siblings and am so grateful to be so richly blessed. My mother gave birth to 10 beautiful and fun new bundles of joy and they were all wanted and welcome, and I have to admit they are so cute! Every one of them! Myself included! LOL (I love myself... I am the best... to hec with him (Lou-or Lucifer).. and all the rest (of his followers). Thank you for giving each of us a solid relationship and understanding that we are children of God and are of a royal heritage. We learned that at a very young age.

Thank you Mom.

I had the coolest mom in the whole world and I got to share her with my friends as she was my Den Mother. She was the best Den Mother in the whole wide world! (at least in my opinion). The world of creation was opened to us and I loved my new pocket knife, that carved out the fantastic and intrique little buffalo soap carving that took 1st place. I would venture to say that it would rival even in the adult world. There were the coolest rockets in the rocket derby which fueled my passions for flying, and the pinewood derby was always a treat.

Dance was kinda fun as my brother was enrolled to help him get a little bit better coordination. I understand a little bit more as Dave turned out to be a GIANT, and it was funny because when we were running together in high school I would have 2 strides to his one. He made it look effortless with those big strides. I had to work twice as hard, but it was so nice to have such a good brother and friend by my side pushing...nope ... wrong word... coasting me to better times and greater heigths. I got to stand on the potium quite a few times.

Music filled our home and I loved when you guys provided us with a guitar and banjo from a Mexico trip. (Along with a fun chess set that we couldn't wait to play our Dad. He was REALLY GOOD! At least we thought so.

I remember when the piano came into the home and it looked too complicated and intimidating. but I remember Mom in her curlers, sitting at the piano and plunking out a toon or too, and eventually getting lessons so that I was amazed at how fast she was able to learn. In short order she was quite a pianist, and by her example of consistency and determination shared her talents with her family. (Thanks to Dad for providing the instruments. I understand it was Dad's idea and just showed up with it one day) Mom asked "Who is this for? cause nobody plays the piano?" Dad's response was, "Somebody will some day."

I think every child can plink out a tune, but most are insanely talented. I have to laugh a little because I am not very good, but who would of ever guessed that I am a piano teacher today, and love to help others learn and grow, and music is such a wonderful way to do that. Especially the piano as it will be beneficial to whatever music direction you go. This gift of music has allowed enjoyment in band, violin, harmonica, trumpet, baritone, recorder, drums, banjo, guitar, ... well I could go on and on. The world is an open book and if it is an instrument, can't hardly hold still. Just like to pick it up and play.

2 things that were definitely **not learned** from Mom was **driving**, and **swimming**.

Mom didn't drive until I was about Jr High age and was kinda forced into it out of necessity as we were building a house, and Grandma needed her to drive. The other was swimming. Now I had a fear of swimming until I got down to Lake Powell with the in-laws and they were all water dogs so one time when we were on the lake, I was told the wet suit I had on was special. It had materials equivelant to a life jacket in it so that I would not sink. I was not concerned that the depth of the lake was hundreds of feet deep because my brother-in-law said you can drown in a bath tub, You'll be okay. It doesn't matter if it is 2 feet, or 200. Just stay on top and breath and you'll be fine.

I jump out of the boat with this "special" wetsuit on and sure enough I can float, so I tell him to go ahead and put my nephew in and I will assist him in getting his skiis on and help him learn to water ski for the first time. Well he got up and down a few times and then they came back and picked me up. When I got in the boat they informed me there was nothing special about the wet suit, and I had been out there treading water the whole time. I freaked out and it was a good thing they waited to tell me after I got in the boat. After this experience they coaxed me to jump off the super high dive, and I looked down at the little people, and said, "I don't swim." They told me " No worries, just hold your breath and you'll float to the top- 2 kicks and your over to the wall. Sure enough, they were right. I lived and even jumped in and learned to SCUBA DIVE.

FATHER

As the world gets busier and noisier, it becomes critical for us to carve out time for those things that are of greatest importance, and from my vantage point My Father always put us at the front of the line whenever there was that option.

Bing a father is the toughest, but most important job I will ever have on this earth.

One day I was having a conversation with a friend that had been through a divorce as well and she shared these thoughts from a woman's vantage point that gave me a new perspective to think about. I had been murmurring a little about monies paid out that I didn't even have, and I greatly appreciated her gentle and kind remarks.

***

She Said,

"I understand the feeling about being just around to make money. Let me just share my feeling about that thought

-I think it comes from the adversary working on fathers. It is not that way.

Without money that family cannot have the physical surroundings to lead a spiritual existence. If a women feels she cannot rely on her spouse for the basics of a roof over the famiys head and food on the table, she has a hard time trusting him in other things. You have no idea how scary it is to have a little one in your arms that needs your mothering and you have no time to hardly think or sleep and then you have to deal with the fact that your spouse won't work. What it feels like is that the family has no provider or protector.

Ive been there more times than I care to think.If you think of the money as providing a foundation of security for those wonderful kids of yours, it will change your viewpoint. Security is what they need from their dad and money is half of the equation. The other is love and it sounds like they let you know that youre doing a good job in that arena. It takes kids feeling secure to get them to feel anchored and trusting in God. This is why the security a father gives to the family by providing a living is so important to the relationship a child has with God.

Your X may learn to appreciate you if she works full time, but she may not too. I dont understand a lot of the craziness women seem to be going through regarding the home and family and Having to work to meet their own needs.

Unless they get some easy job, theyll find its a dog eat dog world. To make enough to support my family, I have spent many years being the only woman in board rooms, the only woman who wasnt invited to the big boy golf tournaments where they decided the fate of my job with their fraternizing. Most of the women who say they want to work, only want an outlet, but they still expect their X or spouse to provide for the family. I wonder how it would feel if they HAD to make enough to support their family.

They would find the work world a bit harsher place. "

*** THANK YOU FATHER

I have found these words to be very helpful in taking care of my family. It was no easy task, and I am quite sure that the people on the other side of the fence were having a hard time understanding what I was going through. This brought great insight.In later years, we recieved further clarification when the **Proclamation to the World"** was released and gives some very important instructions to each family member of responsibilities and duties. I thank my parents for being such good examples and for a father that I NEVER heard complain about his duties as a father., and provided that security to his family in an exemplary way.

We love our parents. dearly. Your lives have blessed our lives! My most favored PIONEERS. Thank you for blazing the TRAIL for us. From all your kids:

WE LOVE YOU!

~MP~
CHAPTER 13

Saving the prophet's father
Matthew Burnett

Contribution- Great Grandpa
Matthew Burnett
- Saving the prophet's father

One of the most well-known stories about Matthew Burnett is how he saved David McKay's (the prophet David O. McKay's father) life. David McKay was heading home to Huntsville one stormy night. The river in Ogden Canyon was very high and swift; the roar was deafening. Brother McKay pulled his team over to let Matthew pass by with his wagon.

David got too close to the edge and the wagon tipped over, dumping him into the swirling waters below. The swift current carried him down, slamming his body into the rocks. He finally caught hold of a large rock in the middle of the river and managed to pull himself up unto it. In the meantime, Matthew Burnett was plodding along, letting the horses have a loose rein because they could pick out the road better than a human in these stormy conditions. He had his coat pulled up and his cap pulled down to keep out the cold. He thought he heard someone, but with the roaring water, he wasn't sure.

A voice came to him and said, "Go back. There is a man in the river." He untied the team, unhooked the mare and returned to where he heard the call. He saw Brother McKay on the rock, waving his arms. The river made a big turn above the rock where the water washed around it, and the bank was very steep. Matthew went up river and made the horse jump in the water. The force of the water carried them downstream to the rock, finally pressing the horse against the rock long enough for Brother McKay to climb on.

As the horse started to swim, the current carried them to bank of the river near the road. The McKay's wagon was nearby with his team standing close to it. Brother McKay later said that when he climbed up on that rock, he knelt and prayed for some way to be rescued. This was the moment that Matthew had heard the voice telling him there was a man in the river.

~MP~
CHAPTER 14

Modern Pioneers- Write you Own Story

COMING TO A BOOK NEAR YOU!

The end

~MINI LIFE LEGACY~
Game

(L&L 20 Questions to build a Strong Story) Only answer the questions with responses you are comfortable in sharing (fun, little snippets that may help others (Avoid negatives unless you have a strong solution, then by all means share!

Powerful!)

After playing & jotting down ideas from the game, a good way to start the

MINI LL is:

Grab a friend and give this a try. Especially if you know someone is struggling. It can give them the opportunity to count their many blessings and realize they are important, and you will have fun enjoying their company

A fun way to write a nice and interesting autobiography. 3-5 pages and your story will be impressive. I encourage you to write it down so the rest of the world can enjoy it.

PROBLEM

A-PROBLEM: Identify common PROBLEM others can relate to and may be struggling with as well

STORY

B-STORY: Tell Brief STORY -(make a connection – but just enough-& not too Graphic-make connection)

SOLUTION

C-SOLUTION -(The SOLUTION you LEARNED or DISCOVERED that helps the reader move forward)

*Your story is GREAT-This is fun with a group of 2 or more people and a little timer***

2 Min. Response time per Q Approximately 1/2 Hr+ or (speed round 15 min.) Jot down /record responses

Lets have FUN!   Thanks for Playing!

***1**-Born and Raised & How you got your name*

***2**-Family: Kids/Bro/Sis Par & Gr/Cousins/Nieces/Nephews/Ancestors/..*

***3**-Holidays/Special Events:*

***4**-Food Favorites-(To Eat &Make) -Recipes*

***5**-Church: callings/leaders/scriptures/conversion story/life tests.*

***6**-Love &Friends: close, old, new, young, financial, gone, Animals / Pets*

***7**-Entertainment/Travel: Travel/Toys/memorabilia/ games /-(night/board/card/movies)*
***8**-Health & Wellness / Illnesses /Meds/ Drs/ Nutra/Pharma/Patients*

***9**-Success &Celebrations/Failures/Problems Solutions, and Learning*
Opportunities/Forgiveness : ex. Child/grownups/ authority/$/friends/law

***10**-Service: Missions / Community / World / Military*

11-Attitudes / Theories / Quotes
_12__-Mentors / Coaches /Talents /Skills/Instruments/Music_

_13__-**Edu**. /Schooling: El, Jr., HS, College, Teachers/Principles/Adm_

_14__- Likes / Dislikes / habits /patterns /exercise /discipline/ affection /Passion_ **(LOVE)**

_15__-Groups & Org.: Running/Band/Scouts/Rep/Dem etc_

_16__-Jobs & Careers / Businesses and Associates /Trade_

_17__-Cars and vehicles owned: motos/snowmobile/boats/tricycles/bikes/wagon_
_18__-What is your Y (What is your purpose- Your mess is your message)_

_19__-**Change**: If you could travel through time (past)P-P-F and change ?_

_20__-What ? Do you need to add to this list to make it complete?_

*ENDING WITH A TESTIMONY OR PERSONAL THOUGHTS IS ALWAYS NICE
copyright GB 2017

Senses: (taste, sight, touch, smell, sound to describe and enhance your story)

Made in the USA
Columbia, SC
09 July 2019